T·H·E RATIONAL I·N·F·A·N·T
Learning in Infancy

·THE·
RATIONAL
Learning in Infancy
I·N·F·A·N·T

T. G. R. Bower
University of Texas — Dallas

91-1419

■■ W. H. Freeman and Company • New York

Library of Congress Cataloging-in-Publication Data

Bower, T. G. R., 1941–
  The rational infant.
  (A Series of books in psychology)
  Bibliography: p.
  Includes index.
  1. Learning, Psychology of.   2. Infant psychology.
I. Title.   II. Series.
BF318.B68   1989   155.4′22   88-31082
ISBN 0-7167-2005-1
ISBN 0-7167-2007-8 (pbk.)

Printed in the United States of America

0 1 2 3 4 5 6 7 8 9   VB   7 6 5 4 3 2 1 0 8 9

Contents

Preface

I began writing and talking about learning nearly eight years ago. I had a number of motives for this. One was simple exasperation. Learning theory was the core of psychology in my own student days. Its perceived importance declined under the impact of modern rationalism on the one hand and on the other, the growing body of data showing that very young infants are more capable than some theories of learning would have us believe. As a result a whole generation of students were unaware of the conceptual advances made by learning theorists. This left a void in the fabric of developmental psychology, a void which was being filled, in some cases, by tentative rediscovery of ideas that were genuinely new in the 1930s. It is pointless to wail that psychology is not a cumulative science if one makes no effort to ensure that it is.

A second motive stemmed from clinical concerns. There are infants who have been damaged in one way or another. Therapy boils down to a manipulation of their environment in some way. To work out what manipulations to do one has to know how the organism, the growing child, uses the information that is provided by the environment. A theory of information use is a theory of learning. It seems to me that there is no hope for an applied developmental psychology without a theory of learning.

My third motive was closer to basic science. I had been working on computer simulations of developmental processes. It was clear by the end of that effort that what was needed was a description of the basic structures that control the utilization of information that is presented to the organism. A description of such structures would be a theory of learning.

My own thoughts on these topics were given a massive jolt by some new ideas advanced by Jean Piaget towards the end of his life. At a stroke it seemed that a suitably modified learning theory could account for the very phenomena that had seemed most recalcitrant to treatment by learning theory.

I would undoubtedly have produced a book on learning and development without the stimulus provided by Piaget. However, whatever novelty this book has is a result of Piaget's ideas. I owe him a great debt for this as well as so many other things. I needed help to make sense of Piaget's ideas. I am deeply grateful to Alan Leslie and Barry Richards who provided that help.

This book is the outcome of a lot of thought and some experimentation. In the course of it I was greatly helped by a number of students, in particular Meryl Hacking, Marjorie Fisher, Fiona Gordon, and John Petrie. Their ingenuity exceeded mine, which is as it should be. I hope their careers flourish as they should.

A substantial part of the text was put in first draft in Japan. I was speaking in English and my translators requested a draft. Since I never normally use notes, much less a text, for lectures, this was a challenge. I thank my friends in Kyoto, particularly Teddy Bear, for their support.

The resulting manuscript was too much a series of written talks. In my own attempt to rewrite, I was greatly helped by Meryl Hacking. The greatest burden fell on my editor at W. H. Freeman. I and my readers owe a great debt to Georgia Lee Hadler for the immense amount of work she put in.

Jennifer Wishart picked up some errors in an early draft, and Gail Walton and Victoria Everhart removed the last ones from the final draft. Vicki also read the proofs, with my help. I thank them both.

The whole manuscript was read and criticized by Andrew Meltzoff and John Watson. I owe them more than I can convey for their sympathetic and constructive criticism.

I hope the book will stimulate some interest in the learning of infants. Babies are very competent. They are set to use whatever information we give them. That I find a sobering thought. What we put in determines what we will get out. If we sow storms, we shall reap whirlwinds.

T. G. R. Bower

T·H·E RATIONAL I·N·F·A·N·T
Learning in Infancy

1

Development — Stable or Unstable?

The subtitle of this book is *Learning in Infancy*. I have been surprised during its writing to have to defend the value of the enterprise. There seems to be a feeling that the interest in infancy has gone far enough. Over the last twenty-five years or so we have learned a great deal about the world of the infant, the nature of the baby's abilities and sensitivities. In a number of recent publications I sense a feeling that some of us now know more about infancy than we ever wanted to and that it is time to turn our attention to something else (see e.g., Kagan, 1984). The role of infancy and experience in infancy, on this view, has been vastly overrated for the last three millenia. It is about that long that we have assumed that experience in infancy had a special role in the history of every human life. "The first step is what matters most when dealing with those who are young and tender — any impression we choose to make leaves a permanent mark" (Plato, *Republic*). This view is definitely under attack. For Kagan (op. cit.) development — the history of a human life — can be viewed as "a traveler whose knapsack is slowly filled with doubts, dogma and desires during the first dozen years. Every traveler spends the adult years trying to empty the heavy load in the knapsack."

On this view, infancy — a mere one or two years of life — can hardly be of special significance. To be sure, we have a moral responsibility to understand the baby's understanding of what is going on — it seems intolerable now that pediatric textbooks until 1963 (e.g., Peiper, 1963) could maintain that infants were insensitive to stimuli that produce anguish in adults. Nonetheless we need not assume that the experiences we impose on infants, however understood, have any special significance. "Any environment will suffice for perfectly normal development," writes Sandra Scarr (1981), dismissing in a moment the whole history of attempts to define the ways in which we should nurture our young so that they will grow to be healthy, happy, and wise.

I must confess that my own first reaction to these ideas was to dismiss them as horsefeathers. Michael Lewis (1982) put it more politely: "[T]his principle — the decreasing importance of experience with increasing age — is not open to denial by fact . . . rather should be taken as a premise."

However, I soon began to worry that my reaction was not well founded, in fact reflected no more than my own conservatism. We need not venerate an idea because it is venerable; antiquity is no guarantee of truth. Certainly the general theory that early experience has disproportionate influence in determining the flow of a human life has some corollaries that are true now but were ridiculous one hundred years ago. Bowlby (1951) has promoted the idea that a stable, caring mother-infant relationship is essential to the development of a stable, caring person. The idea is very widely accepted. It would have seemed absurd to Charles Dickens. His character, Oliver Twist, had the very opposite of a stable, caring relationship with anyone in his early childhood. A modern novelist, familiar with Bowlby, would probably make a sadistic psychopath of Oliver, certainly not the sweet-natured sop of Dickens's creation. Are Bowlby's ideas "true," or are they merely extensions of an antique theory that is due for revision? Is it the case that we have been programmed to see connections where none exist?

I must also confess that I am tempted by the idea that our infantile past does not determine our present or our future, tempted in the same way as I am by books and films where, with one bound, our hero is free. Nonetheless it still seems there is some evidence that would predispose a naive observer to believe that early experience does have more potent effects than later experience.

Above we referred to Bowlby's perhaps controversial views on the disproportionate significance of early caretaking for the development of personality. Bowlby's core idea that it is essential for the infant to have full-time maternal care on a one-to-one basis has been seen by many as a manifestation of the male chauvinist plot to curtail the freedom of woman. Perhaps for that reason the idea has been subjected to extremely severe scrutiny. Bowlby's idea, put simply, is that the baby's first experiences of other humans will shape and determine all possible later relationships. Bleak outcomes are possible. Bowlby's own nightmare is the affectionless character, or psychopath, the individual who may charm on the surface but is forever remote from normal human feeling, able on occasion to perpetrate cruelties that seem unspeakable to normal individuals. The affectionless character, the psychopath, is, for Bowlby, the outcome of inconsistent patterns of care in infancy. Such a child, adopted into a stable, loving home, would remain trapped by the past, unable to enjoy or return love, or so Bowlby has predicted. Propitious outcomes are also possible, in theory, if the child has had stable care in infancy. Such children, according to Bowlby, are buffered against all the blows that life can hurl, growing inevitably into stably affectionate adults.

Bowlby's ideas were controversial throughout the 1950s. As a young student I attended a conference where Bowlby was the main speaker; the audience did not throw beer cans at him, but it was a near thing. Acceptance, or even evaluation, of his ideas was not made easier by the overenthusiasm of some of his acolytes. One eminent scientist, her own child-rearing days well behind her, roundly condemned any mother who read in the presence of her baby, thereby visiting a measure of maternal deprivation on her hapless infant. Despite the kerfuffle, the balance of evidence does support Bowlby, if not his wilder followers. His own review was massively well documented. A review by Rutter (1981), emphasizing that benign later

3

circumstances can have a positive effect, nonetheless concludes that "the first few years do have a special importance for bond formation and social development" (p. 18).

It is possible to discern a general acceptance of Bowlby's views among the caring professions. Continuity of maternal care is now seen as a prime aim, even when the material quality of the care is poor enough to have required the intervention of some welfare agency. This means, fortunately for society, that Bowlby's main contribution to theory is becoming untestable. Bowlby wrote about the malign effects of deprivation of maternal care. At the time, the world was full of abandoned children, a consequence of the war. The law courts thought nothing of separating mother and baby, as did the medical profession. Given peace and Bowlby's own efforts, the population of deprived children has become so small that further testing has become impossible. He pointed out one instance where early experience seems to have a disproportionate effect, an effect that is not reversed by years of contrary experience. This is accepted by the population at large, even though the mediating mechanisms are not well understood by psychologists. We are talking here about an effect of early experience, mediated in some fashion by processes of learning, in infancy.

A second area of investigation, where there does seem to be agreement, concerns the effects of early blindness. Congenital blindness has malign effects that are not at all visible in children blinded after a sighted infancy; the absence of sight in infancy thus has a malign effect. The malign effects are various. One possible outcome is that sight restoration surgery becomes a useless procedure, a medical success, a neurophysiological success, but not a functional success (Senden, 1956; Valvo, 1971).

There are less spectacular but still significant effects. For example the congenitally blind child's understanding of spatial relations diverges more and more with increasing age from that of the sighted child (Figure 1-1). In adolescence congenitally blind children may fail completely to understand what teachers and examiners want them to understand in geometry (Drever, 1955). However the blind child construes his world, Euclidean geometry does not offer him a formal system that is at all comprehensible. Children blinded after infancy cannot be differentiated in this way. Some indeed have become famous geometers, for example, Peterson, described by Drever (op. cit.). There is a clear symmetry here with the effects of caring style.

4

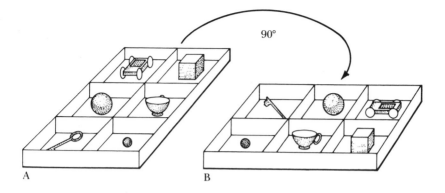

Figure 1-1 On this task blind children become progressively worse with age relative to sighted children. A child is presented with a partitioned box of toys (A). He is then given a duplicate set of toys and asked to put these in the identical arrangement in another box turned 90° from the position of the first box (B). The task is then repeated, reversing the orientations of the model box and test box. (From Bower, 1979; adapted from Hatwell, 1974.)

An environmental circumstance in infancy has an effect, benign or malign, that cannot be reversed by the opposite circumstance, whether benign or malign, even though the opposing circumstance operates for years longer than the initial disposing circumstance. We have here another instance of the disproportionate effects of early experience, mediated by processes of learning, in infancy.

There is a third possible instance of early environmental influence. Every year there are a number of individuals born who, for a variety of reasons, must grow up with a gender assignment that contradicts their genetic makeup. There is a very obvious genetic difference between men and women. Every cell in our bodies contains our own individual genetic complement, thousands upon thousands of genes, arranged in packets, chromosomes, which are in turn arranged in pairs, 22 pairs, with a final pair X and X in women and X and Y in men (Figure 1-2). The XX versus XY difference seems so clearly correlated with the behavioral and psychological differences between women and men that many have asserted that the genetic difference causes the behavioral and psychological difference.

For reasons ranging from surgical error (e.g., during circumcision) to biochemical accidents of great complexity, some individuals are given a contrary label or are in error "mislabeled," in genetic terms.

5

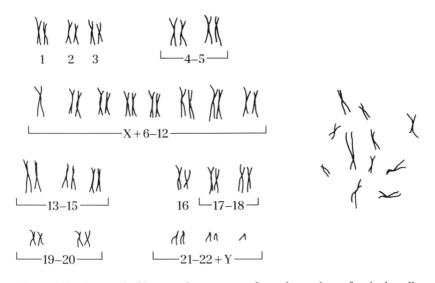

Figure 1-2 A spread of human chromosomes from the nucleus of a single cell, and their classified arrangement or karyotype. The presence of the X and Y chromosomes signifies the male genotype, X and X the female. Each chromosome contains thousands of genes. The genetic difference between male and female is thus very large. (Adapted from Money and Ehrhardt, 1972.)

This means that some individuals with an X and Y chromosome will be labeled female, while some who are XX will be labeled male. "Maleness" and "femaleness" cover a whole range of behaviors. Individuals who have been cross-labeled show the behavior patterns appropriate to the label, not those appropriate to their chromosomes. The label can be "corrected," a reassignment of gender can be made, but "the age ceiling for an imposed reassignment is, in the majority of cases, around eighteen months" (Money and Ehrhardt, 1972). Gender, a system of behaving as a female or as a male, is pretty much fixed thereafter. The system of behaving may be at odds with the biology of the individual, biology at the most basic level. It is a psychological system, quite independent of the biological structures that it will use. Clearly once again we are dealing with the powerful effects of early experience, mediated by processes of learning, in infancy.

A last possible instance I must mention has to do with the effect of early learning on later learning ability. There has been controversy over whether early practice in learning can facilitate later learning in

6

new situations. The U.S. government, in the 1960s, began a program of compensatory education, the Head Start program, on the assumption that the proposition was true. There was at that time, and still is, a strong body of evidence that would support the idea. Rutter (op. cit.), in his large-scale review, summarizes the data on the possibility of countering the malign effects of an environment with restricted possibilities for learning: "Considerable reversal of cognitive ill-effects is possible with a complete and permanent change of environment, *provided that this occurs in infancy* . . . extensive reversal is usual, if the change . . . *occurs during infancy*." As for the effect of a sudden restriction on children who had had a good environment for learning, he writes "the older the child . . . the less the retardation." Thus lack of opportunity for learning in infancy has a malign effect that can be reversed by intervention in infancy; opportunity for learning has a benign effect that will buffer the child against the effects of future privations.

These conclusions are in no way affected by the mixed results of Head Start. The average Head Start project gave six weeks of environmental enrichment to children who were three years of age at the time. It is a wonder that anyone could have supposed that this would produce major effects. It is more wonderful yet that some long-term effects were produced (Darlington et al., 1980). It is only by understanding the process of early learning that we can hope to undo the malign effects of early experience in any reliable way. To preserve that optimism we must accept learning as a mediator and look at how it works.

With this last instance, or possible instance, of the effects of early experience, we are approaching the central fascination of studies of learning in infancy, the epistemological fascination, our own curiosity about the origins of our whole system of knowledge and belief. There is a longstanding theory that roots all of human knowledge in learning, that denies there is any knowledge that is built into the structure of the human organism, save the knowledge required for learning itself. To be able to prove that the ability to learn was itself dependent on prior experience would surely complete the sceptical essay against innate ideas, blasting apart any speculation that any human knowledge comes with our structure, in the same way as breathing does. This issue has fascinated humans for thousands of years and it is only the study of learning in infancy that can resolve it.

7

Thus far I have said nothing about what I mean by learning. For the moment I shall equate the term with "detection of a contingent relation between events," with "noticing that one event follows another," and thereby coming to expect the second, given the first. This definition is broad enough to cover the standard psychological usage. The events in question are of course events as perceived by the organism. No organism could connect events that it could not register. A preliminary to a study of learning in infants is thus a definition of the perceptual world of the infant, the topic of our next chapter.

2

The Perceptual World

For the last twenty-five years, infants in growing numbers have been participating in experiments designed to let adults find out how they, the infants, perceive the world around them. The basic question we have asked has always been the same: is their world like our world, or is it completely different? There was always an assumption, explicit or implicit, that the differences, if any, would be of a particular kind, manifesting a lack or insufficiency on the part of the infant. I worked in that framework myself for many years. If forced to specify the lack I was looking for, I guess I would say that I was looking for evidence that infants fail to make the distal projections that we adults do. "Distal projection" does not trip as lightly off the tongue as some other phrases we might find in a textbook of perception. Nonetheless I think it describes the core problem in the psychology of perception, the problem of how it is that we are aware of a world of objects arrayed around and away from us in sometimes distant places; that is, our world. We are mostly unaware of another possible world where we would be conscious of the flux of energy at our receptors, a world within our heads, rather than ranged in space about us. We adults can occasionally become aware of the proximal flux that is there at our sense organs. For example, at least part of art school training is training to become aware of the light at our receptors, rather than the world specified by that light (Figure 2-1). Some adults spontaneously find themselves afloat in a proximal flux. Békésy (1967) describes one such case from his youth. He writes:

> At the time when I was a beginning communications engineer, earphones were always used in listening to the radio. One day an important politician came to the laboratory bitterly complaining that while listening to music on the radio he heard the entire orchestra in his head. His wife had a solution to the problem, which was to visit a psychiatrist. This would have had serious political consequences, and instead he asked me to repair his radio. The problem, which was solved in a two-hour session is illustrated in Figure [2-2]. If a person has an earphone on each ear and the two are well matched the acoustical situation provides a free choice of localizing the imaged sound source in front, within the head, or behind. The determining condition will probably be some early experience relative to this situation. For the patient's cure he was asked to sit in front of a sound source, which he localized correctly in front. Then he was asked to put his two hands in front of the ear openings and to flap them back and forth. After a while, with the proper hand positions, he was able to hear the sound in the back of his head, and then he could make the sound change its position

Figure 2-1   The production of a two-dimensional image of three dimensions, like the one shown here, is a skill that takes years to acquire.

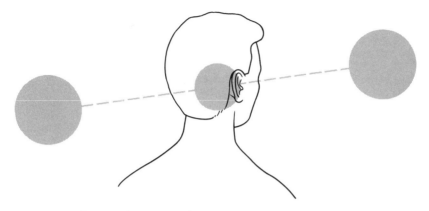

Figure 2-2   The ambiguous localization of a sound listened to with a pair of earphones. (Adapted from Békésy, 1967.)

from one place to the other. We then used the visual situation of Figure [2-3] to explain that he had three choices in his perception of the figure. In a short time the person had no difficulty in locating the orchestra in front or behind, as he pleased, and his problem was solved.

The essence of this case is that stimulation was sensed within the body, rather than being projected out to represent the big, wide world beyond our skin. Without distal projection there is no "out there," no near, no far, not much of a right and left, even. This is the world we thought the baby lived in, a world very different from our own. The problem for scientists was how to find out whether or not the baby engaged in distal projection, at what age the growing child began distal projection, and what experiences and how much of them were necessary for distal projection to begin.

I have thus far used "distal projection" in a restricted, almost literal manner. Detecting the emotion that underlies a pattern of facial expression would be an example of a more extended use of the term. Within the restricted use of the term, how can we know whether or not a baby lives in a three-dimensional world, like us, or in a world without spatial order, a proximal flux?

Two search paradigms have been used, one based on the use of natural functional responses, the other on discriminative responses. While literature on the latter is larger, I shall begin with the former. In examining any organism, we have a habit of comparing that organism's behavior in a given situation with our own behavior in the

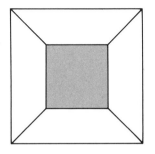

Figure 2-3 Ambiguous figure, used by Bekesy. (Adapted from Békésy, 1967.)

same situation. If the responses are identical, we tend to assume that the organism in question perceives the world just as we do. If the responses differ in some systematic way, we tend to assume that there is a systematic difference in the perceptual worlds that generate the responses.

Since young infants do not have an obvious vast repertoire of acts, there have not been a great many studies that have used natural responses to index the perceptual world of the infant. One of the first such studies and certainly, in its time, a heroic study, concerned the very form of distal projection that occupied Békésy — auditory localization. We normally hear sound emanating from specific locations in space. As we saw, this kind of distal projection can fail. Does the infant make the distal projection or not?

Wertheimer (1961) was fortunate enough to gain access to a delivery room to carry out his experiment. His subject was delivered without anaesthesia (an important point), and the birth was free from trauma. Having thus obtained an optimal subject, Wertheimer presented a series of sounds, randomly to the right or left of the subject. Over the initial period, before boredom set in, the subject correctly looked in the direction of the sound source. There can be no doubt that the initial localizing attempts of this infant, tested almost at the moment of birth, were nonrandom and were in fact quite accurate in direction, qualifying as evidence of distal projection.

This result has been replicated by a number of experimenters who have supplied us with more data on early auditory localization. It is now clear that, by a few days after birth, infants are capable of more than right-straight ahead-left discrimination; degrees of rightness and leftness can be discriminated. The way in which this is manifested is quite fascinating and has considerable implication for research techniques. Essentially these results show that if a major effort is required to fixate a sound source — a head movement and an eye movement — then the more effort required, the less likely are infants to make an orienting response (MacFarlane, 1977). The technical implication is that studies of auditory localization should not use extreme stimulus positions if they wish to demonstrate localization. An experiment that used only extreme positions might conclude, erroneously, that newborns cannot localize sounds. An example of this kind of error is the study by McGurk et al. (1977), which used only stimuli 90° off the midline, the position least likely to elicit looking behavior. As a result, the researchers concluded, unjustifiably, that infants 2 to 8 days old cannot localize sounds.

Additional complications for research techniques have also been introduced in studies that used the human voice as a stimulus. Quite soon after birth, bottle-fed infants will begin to turn their heads away from a voice source, while breast-fed infants continue to turn toward a sound source. These opposed behaviors are surely the result of the differential link between the voice source and food in the breast or bottle situation. The breast is always on the same side as the voice in breast-feeding, while the bottle is normally in the opposite direction during bottle-feeding. As soon as the infant learns this, use of a voice stimulus could indicate — or, rather, might be interpreted as indicating — that the infant's auditory localization is totally inaccurate, again a conclusion that would be quite unwarranted (Alegria and Noirot, 1978).

Lastly, Turkewitz et al. (1966) found that looking responses to sound sources, like looking responses to light sources, are a function of the intensity of the stimulus. If the stimulus is very intense, looking away is more likely than looking toward — a clearly adaptive response (see also Butterworth and Castillo, 1976).

While this brief history of how we established that newborn infants do project sounds to distal locations, is informative in itself, it also throws light on the problems faced by investigators of the early abilities of human beings. Wertheimer dared to suggest that a newborn human could actually respond in a distally appropriate manner. The suggestion met with a great deal of opposition. I have no doubt that the opposition was fueled by the numerous tomes outlining theories of how the newborn could learn how to localize sounds. If the newborn could localize anyway, the labor of constructing and learning such theories could be seen to be in vain.

If one is determined that infants of some age can do nothing, then it is extremely easy to fail to find evidence that they *do* do something. The baby is temperamental and difficult enough that failures of this kind are child's play. (I would go so far as to say that anyone can fail to replicate any claim that young infants can do anything.) One, of course, then has a duty to provide an explanation of the difference between the original and the failed replication. By explaining a failure to replicate we can advance our understanding. Hayes and Watson (1981) is a model example.

The change of view on this issue is witnessed by the auditory abilities currently being attributed to the newborn or days-old infant — such as the ability to identify and discriminate speech sounds and the patterning of a language (Mehler, 1986). In the light of current claims, the controversy over auditory localization seems silly. However, it had to be resolved before today's experiments could even be thought of.

The next indicator behavior, reaching, is, I would say, at the same state of resolution, although to some it is still controversial. It is not at all controversial to say that infants begin to reach in the second half of the first year. However, to say that they begin to do so soon after birth, *is*. When parents told me that their babies could reach soon after birth, for years my reaction was to pat them on the head (metaphorically in most cases) and say, "Yes, your baby is wonderful!"

I was so convinced that the textbooks were right and that reaching began at about five months — not five days — that I simply paid no attention to such reports. I was finally convinced that they had some substance when I saw my own nephew display this behavior at three weeks of age; and again when a child of a colleague (not about to be put off by polite skepticism) also did so at the age of only one week. It was only after these parents had alerted me to this behavior that I even noticed it, despite the fact that I had been working intensively with babies in this age range for several years.

In looking at infant behavior, scientists, as much as anyone else, tend to be blinded by their preconceptions about what the organism can and cannot do. They look for what they expect to see, rather than looking straightforwardly at what the organism actually does.

Reaching is at first sight a perfect indicator of distal projection. The hand moves out to an object, to a location away from the baby. There is no reason to suppose this would occur without distal projection.

14

The behavior of course is not leapingly obvious. Bower, Broughton, and Moore (1970b), who did the first systematic studies, specified a number of conditions for its appearance. The behavior was most likely to be seen in babies who had been born naturally, and was very unlikely to be seen in babies who had undergone a high-tech birth. It was important that the babies were in a position where they could reach; for example, that their hands and arms were free (Bower, 1974, 1982). We suggested ways to ensure babies could reach, specifying a particular set of body positions. Lastly we specified that the babies should be young, since the behavior, for whatever reasons, becomes less probable with increasing age. We also specified that the babies should be awake.

Casting an undoubtedly jaundiced eye over the purported replications of our study, I can barely find one that paid any attention to our precautionary notes. Despite all of this, however, there were some positive notes sounded. Butterworth (1978) did write:

> In my own laboratory, we allow two hours to obtain a five-minute video recording of one infant reaching. Most of the time is spent ensuring that the baby is in the optimal condition to display the behavior, if he (or she) is going to. We have the mother feed and change the baby at the lab and generally ensure that the infant is wide awake. Having taken these precautions, there is little doubt that infants in the first few weeks of life can reach toward and sometimes grasp objects on which they fixate visually.

Subsequently a number of authors have reported positive results, that infants a few days of age will in fact extend their hands toward a visible object (Trevarthen et al., 1975; McDonnell, 1979; Rader and Stern, 1982; Schonen, 1980; Fontaine, 1984), indeed, even to a visible moving object (Hofsten, 1980). Rader and Stern (op. cit.) pointed out that the criterion of reaching was important. They also showed that the probability of response declines with age between eight and fourteen days of age. The role of posture has also been explicated (Amiel-Tison and Grenier, 1980) in sufficient detail that Fontaine (op. cit.) has been able to elicit very satisfactory reaching from infants in a sitting position; for this to be possible the head must be supported in a particular way (Figure 2-4), relatively fixed, and with some of its weight taken off the spinal column. The newborn head is proportionately very heavy in comparison with the adult head

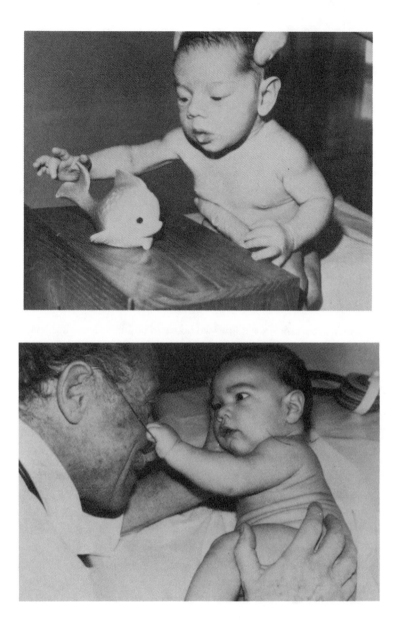

Figure 2-4 When the newborn does not have to worry about the weight of his or her head, very skilled behavior will be demonstrated. (A) Seventeen days old. (B) Two months old. (From Amiel-Tison and Grenier, 1980.)

so that those experimenters who simply place newborns into chairs without support are imposing upon the infants a terrible problem of postural control. To get some idea of what the baby is going through, try attaching weights to your head to bring it to one-third of your body weight. Make sure the weight is above the junction of head and neck. To get a proper comparison you should either perch on a slippery narrow ledge or straddle a slippery beam with your feet dangling in the air in both cases. There are experimenters who have put babies in analogous situations.

While most attention has been given to the mere fact of behavior, some attention has been paid to distal variation. Thus, reaching becomes less likely, the further away the presented object, regardless of its size. This emphasizes the distal nature of infant perception, since in the proximal flux, a ball of 1-inch diameter at 5 inches distance produces the same effect as a 3-inch ball at 15 inches distance — obviously, since distance is not a proximal quality (Figure 2-5). A baby who perceived the proximal flux would be as likely to reach for a small, near object as for a large, far object.

Since infants will reach for the former but not for the latter (Bower, 1971; Butterworth, op. cit.), I would suggest that the world of the newborn is not that of proximal flux: their world does have distal projection; they are aware of different distances.

In the present context, a book on learning in infancy, the most interesting study of neonate reaching is that of Schonen (1980) who found that some experience was necessary if reaching was to occur. The nature of that experience is not at present clear. It is certainly

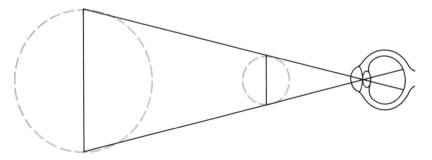

Figure 2-5   In the proximal flux, a ball of 1-inch diameter at 5 inches distance produces the same effect as a 3-inch ball at 15 inches distance.

not the piecemeal coordination of acts to stimuli and consequences imagined by some authors (e.g., White and Held, 1966).

The fracas over neonate reaching seems to be pretty much over. As an instance of sensory motor coordination it pales beside subsequent discoveries, particularly the discovery of the newborn's ability to imitate (Meltzoff and Moore, 1975, 1977, 1983), an ability that is clearly highly complex. Imitation itself caused an immense furor with articles appearing as recently as 1984 with titles like "Do Newborn Infants Really Imitate?" Given that mothers from Scotland to Seattle, Kyoto (Ikegami, 1984) to Nepal (Reissland, 1986) would answer yes, I trust that before long these "experts" will fall into line.

Few other natural responses have been used to index the perceptual world of the newborn. One other I should mention is the infant's response to an approaching object. Bower, Broughton, and Moore (1970a) presented evidence that infants only days of age showed a characteristic pattern of behavior when an object approached their faces, a pattern that could be called defensive. The full pattern (Figure 2-6) included head retraction, eye widening, interposition of hands between face and object, and finally, a blink.

There were a number of procedural points important for the elicitation of the behavior, mostly to do with the posture. They have been described in the original paper and in Bower, 1974. There was one important and neglected feature mentioned in the original. The full-scale response was elicited by a real object that was really moving towards the baby's face. The event produced a complex of changes in stimulation, optical expansion, an air current against the face, and a changing rumble as the object ran along its track. Bower, Broughton, and Moore (op. cit.) presented a pure visual change on its own, utilizing a shadow caster; it produced a delayed and attenuated version of the response to the real object. Air movement by itself did not produce the response at all. We did not present the sound change alone. Subsequent research has concentrated on the visual presentation alone. The results have mostly been positively supportive (e.g., Ball and Tronick, 1971; Yonas et al. 1979).

In an earlier paper (1977), Yonas and his colleagues could not find any evidence of any defensive response in young infants. Since the infants were supported at the waist only, it is hardly surprising that this was so. A very young baby held by the waist as in Yonas's experiment is hardly in a position to do much in the way of defensive movements.

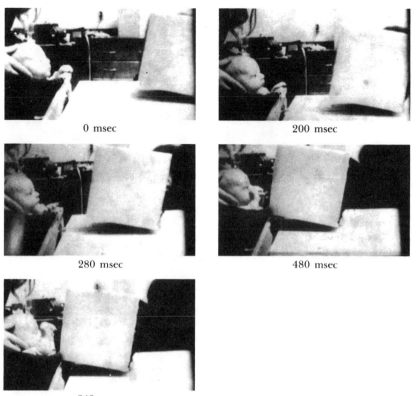

0 msec   200 msec

280 msec   480 msec

840 msec

Figure 2-6 Defensive behavior of a ten-day-old infant elicited by an approach-ing object. The defensive behavior has four clear components: a widening of the eyes, head retraction, interposition of the hands between the face and object and a blink. This response is specific to the distance traveled by the object and not its size. (From Bower, 1971.)

That said, it still seems that the real presentation produced a bigger and better effect. This could indicate some very early form of intersensory coordination or cooperation, just as do the two other behaviors we have considered. At the time all this research began, intersensory coordination was the last thing anyone would have ex-pected to find in the young infant, and yet all of the behaviors we have looked at do seem to involve intersensory coordination.

Since this book is on learning in infancy, I must mention that the response we have been discussing could very well be a learned response. Since the ability is present at one week, it seems likely that

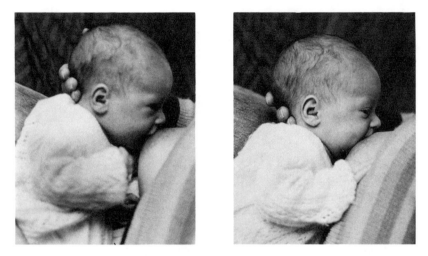

Figure 2-7   An overenthusiastic mother can produce a defensive response to the breast. (Photographs by Jane Dunkeld.)

it is an unlearned ability. However, we cannot be certain. In Bower (1974), I argued that a learning theory explanation was implausible. How many times, I argued, has a one-week-old-infant been struck in the face by an approaching object. A series of letters convinced me to the contrary. During breast-feeding the infant of an inexperienced mother is quite likely to be struck in the face; indeed, overenthusiastic application of the breast can result in a response not unlike that elicited by an approaching object (Figure 2-7) (Gunther, 1961). It is possible that the response to an approaching object is learned on the basis of experience with the breast. Such an argument, however, would not explain the behavior of bottle-fed babies. On the whole, I would prefer to conclude that these experiments do demonstrate a built-in capacity for perception of the third dimension.

Discrimination and identification experiments are very common in psychology. They do not at first sight seem to be the ideal weapons for an assault on the problem of whether or not infants are capable of distal projection. In terms of the subject matter of this chapter, the starting point of infant perception, they must also seem somewhat out of place since they all depend on learning. In essence, in all the experiments I shall discuss, the infant is taught something and then given a transfer task to see what he or she learned in the original task. The training at least removes the child from any literal starting point.

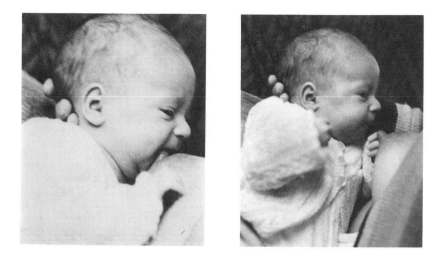

As a paradigm, let us consider size constancy, the ability to detect that an object retains the same size despite a change in its distance from the observer (Figure 2-8). In one variant of the experimental paradigm I am talking about, the baby could be presented with an object of size X at distance Y, producing the proximal flux a retinal image of size Z. The baby could be taught that whenever that object was present an act of his would produce an interesting consequence in the world. When the baby had been taught to respond, one could introduce various transfer conditions.

The amount of transfer, we would suppose, would be a function of the perceived similarity between the conditional situation C and the transfer situation T. Suppose we have the following three transfer situations, T_1, an object of size X is presented at distance $3Y$, producing a retinal image of size $.33Z$; T_2, an object of size $3X$ at distance Y producing a retinal image of size $3Z$; T_3, an object of size $3X$ at distance $3Y$ producing a retinal image of size Z. Figure 2-8 illustrates these experimental conditions.

Now if the infant operates with distal projection, it is surely clear that there would be a hierarchy of probability of response elicitation, with C, the original situation, most likely to elicit responses. T_1 and T_2 each retain one distal feature of C and suffer change in another; a priori they should be equivalent and less effective than C.

T_3 is different in both size and distance and so should be the least effective elicitor if the baby perceives the world in distal terms. If the baby perceives the world with distal projection, there should be a

21

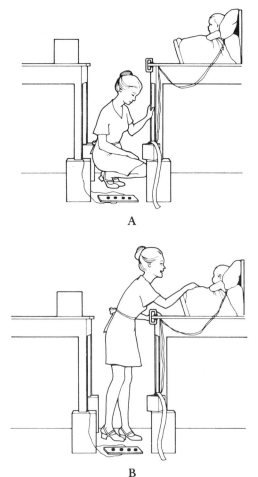

A

B

Figure 2-8 Bower investigated size constancy by using cubes of different sizes placed at different distances from the infants. The conditional stimulus was a 30-centimeter cube at 1 meter distance, and the test stimuli were 30- or 90-centimeter cubes at a distance of 1 or 3 meters away. (A) The experimental setup. The experimental procedure began with conditioning, and the response was reinforced by a "peekaboo" (B). The conditioned response, head turning, closed a microswitch that operated a recorder. After training, a screen was placed between the infant and the stimulus area each time the stimulus object was changed. (Drawings after photographs by Sol Medrick).

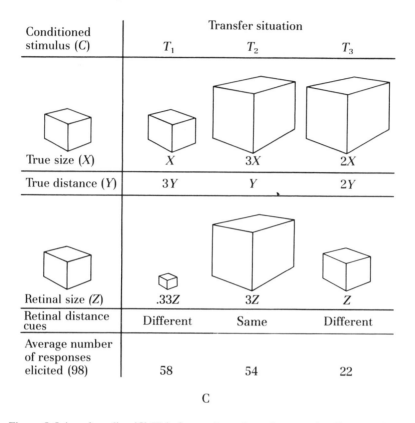

Conditioned stimulus (C)	Transfer situation		
	T_1	T_2	T_3
True size (X)	X	3X	2X
True distance (Y)	3Y	Y	2Y
Retinal size (Z)	.33Z	3Z	Z
Retinal distance cues	Different	Same	Different
Average number of responses elicited (98)	58	54	22

C

Figure 2-8 (continued)   (C) This figure shows how the test stimuli were related to the conditioned stimulus in various respects and the results obtained. From these results it would seem reasonable to conclude that distance perception contributes to the discriminations shown. (Bower, 1966. Copyright © 1966 by Scientific American, Inc. All rights reserved.)

hierarchy of responses so that $C > T_1 = T_2 > T_3$. If, on the other hand, the infant's perceptual world is an image of proximal flux, then the only important changes would be changes in retinal image size, so that the hierarchy would be $C = T_3 > T_1 = T_2$. One or other of these patterns must be obtained.

On no theory of perception is any third pattern predicted. This last point is important so please ponder it.

The same paradigm in essence can be employed using *habituation* rather than operant learning. In the operant learning paradigm outlined above, the baby learns that something interesting will happen in the C situation. In habituation the baby learns that nothing whatsoever will happen in the C situation. The more different a situation is from C, after habituation learning the more the baby will be on the lookout for something to happen. This alerting can be measured. As before, there should be one hierarchy of attention if the baby has distal projection and another if the baby has not. If the baby does project distally, the hierarchy should be $C < T_1 = T_2 < T_3$. If the baby operates in terms of the proximal flux, the hierarchy should be $C = T_3 < T_1 = T_2$. Once again no other outcomes are predicted.

Early results using the operant paradigm supported the hypothesis of distal projection, both for size constancy and shape constancy (Bower, 1966).

Later work using the habituation paradigm also has eventually supported the distal projection hypothesis (e.g., MacKenzie, Tootell, and Day, 1980; Caron, Caron, Carlson, and Cobb, 1979) even for. infants in the first few days of life (Slater and Wood, 1986). So far as I know, no study has ever presented evidence that would support the idea that infants live in the world of proximal flux.

Recall that a properly done experiment must show either that the infant is aware of distal variables or that the infant is aware of only proximal variables. There have in the past been a number of indeterminate studies, a tribute to the difficulty of the experimentation involved. That era now seems to be over. Experiments of this kind are now being used to show that infants can visually detect such distal variables as causality (Leslie and Bower, 1981; Leslie, 1984), gender (Kujawski, 1985), and many others. Again these complex attributions might not be made today if the initial claims about simple projections — size, shape, distance — had not been made and defended.

The work reviewed here in outline or detail is, I think, disquieting to psychologists of my generation. The more the perceptual world of the young infant is investigated the more competent the infant seems to be. And yet we know that there is a great deal of postnatal growth in the perceptual system, a great increment of units in the neural substructure available to process perceptual inputs (Changeux, 1985). What is all this growth for, if the young infant is so capable before it has happened? I intend to argue that behavior equivalent to our own could be mediated by a phenomenal world that is very different from our own. It seems to me possible, despite accumulating data, that the world of the young infant is neither like ours nor any other world we have heretofore imagined. We have tended to suppose that the newborn lives in a world of isolated sensory experiences — sounds, touches, lights — with no given connection in space or time. Extreme proponents of this view, as I was twenty years ago, have even argued that the components of a single object are seen in isolation, as separate fragments as in Figure 2-9 (Bower, 1966; Cohen and Gelber, 1975). Some theorists (e.g., Werner, 1948) have wished to complicate this already confusing world by endowing the newborn child with synaesthesia, so that sound will elicit hallucinatory visual experiences, for example, as well as the proper auditory responses.

My own current view of the newborn's perceptual world is very different. I would argue that the newborn does not respond to sensory experiences as such, indeed is probably unaware of the sensory qualities of stimulation. Instead, I would maintain, the newborn responds to the formal, abstract properties of stimulation, properties which are independent of any specific sense, what Gibson (1950) called higher-order variables. The simplest example of such a variable is provided by those inputs that specify the radial direction of a source of stimulation. Consider a sound source. If straight ahead, a sound source produces exactly the same stimulation at each ear; if it is to the right the right ear is stimulated earlier and more intensely than the left ear; if it is to the left, the opposite happens. In this case symmetry of stimulation equals "straight ahead," asymmetry "off-straight ahead." At a formal level the same system operates for

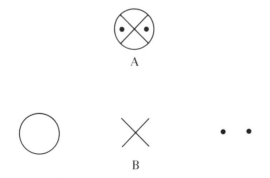

Figure 2-9   Bower's (1966) experiment: (A) The conditioned stimulus was an abstract display. (B) Each of the three test stimuli was a component of the original conditioned stimulus. (From Bower, 1979.)

detection of an olfactory source, a vibratory source and, I have argued, for a visual source. Symmetry-asymmetry of stimulation is independent of any specific modality; it is thus a genuine high-order variable. I am proposing that the newborn responds to these formal, higher-order properties of stimulation, not the sensory inputs that mediate them.

While there is certainly evidence that newborns do pick up and respond to symmetry-asymmetry, the most compelling evidence of response to formal properties of stimulation utilizes an artificial sensory surrogate, the sonic guide. Its main features are summarized in Figure 2-10. As can be seen there, the machine, at a formal level, can present the same information as vision, through a different modality. The signal I wish to focus on is that generated by an approaching object. An approaching object to the eye generates the optical expansion pattern (Figure 2-11), a purely visual signal. That signal, however, can be looked at as a changing pattern over time (Lee and Lishman, 1977), as shown in Figure 2-12. This last pattern, at a formal level, can be mimicked precisely by the sonic guide.

The question is, can the young infant detect and respond to the form of stimulation? The experiments we did (Aitken, 1981) aimed to answer this question and also look at the role of learning in response to approaching objects. The apparatus we used allowed us to vary the sonic guide signal independent of "reality." The experiments were run in darkness. The information presented was thus confined to the sonic guide signal and the air displacement produced by the moving object, ending in slight contact with the baby's face. In one condition, these two signals were consonant, both indicating approach or withdrawal; in the other, they were dissonant, the sonic guide indicating approach while in reality the object receded from the baby's face, and vice versa. The dependent measure which was taken was backward head-pressure (Dunkeld and Bower, 1980).

The results indicated that the sonic guide signal was more important even than contact in determining head retraction (Figure 2-13). It is important to remember that the sonic guide provides a signal to the infant that, at a sensory level, is novel in the experience of the individual and, indeed, of the species. The form of the stimulation, however, is the same familiar form as that provided by vision. The efficacy of the sonic guide information surely attests that young infants are sensitive to the *form* of stimulation rather than its sensory

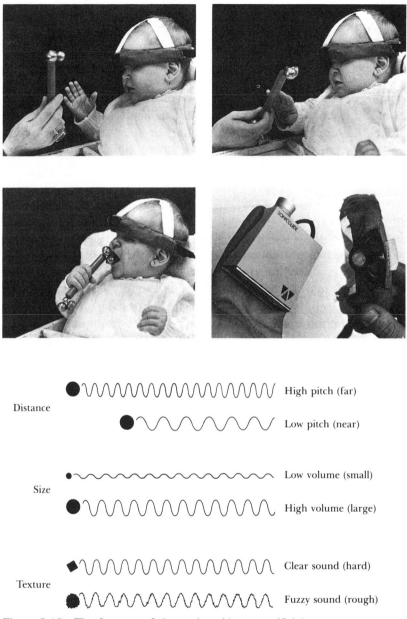

Figure 2-10   The features of the sonic guide, an artificial sensory surrogate. (From Bower, 1974, 1982.)

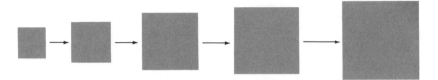

Figure 2-11   The optical expansion pattern generated by an approaching object.

content, the formal properties of stimulation rather than the fragments of sense-data whose arrangement constitutes that form.

I must also point out that these formal properties of stimulation are quite sufficient to support normal perceptual-motor development. I have worked with a number of congenitally blind babies. If provided with the sonic guide when they are young enough, they grow like sighted children, showing none of the lesions of development that usually characterize the blind child. One child shown on television (Bower, 1984), began using the guide when she was about six months old. She is totally blind. At the time the program was made she was twenty-two months old. As viewers could see she shows none of the terrified immobility customarily seen in blind children of her age. If anything she also is cognitively advanced, having solved all of the Piagetian tasks that would normally occupy the first two years of a sighted child's life. In language, even before two years of age she

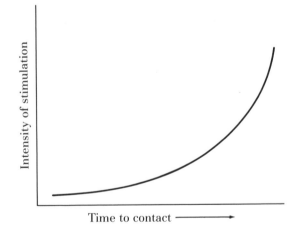

Figure 2-12   The approach of an object can be represented as a change in stimulation over time.

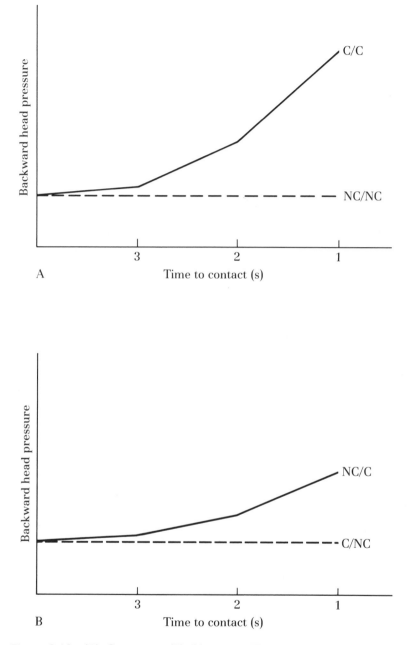

Figure 2-13 (A) Consonant. (B) Dissonant. The broken line = sonic guide indicates withdrawal; the solid line = sonic guide indicates approach.

29

was using prepositions correctly, unusual in a sighted child, even less usual in a blind child. Formal, abstract higher-order variables, variables whose sensory content is novel to us as a species, can thus support a normal program of development, evidence surely that these variables *are* the starting point for development.

The most compelling evidence that newborns elaborate their view of the world on the basis of formal properties comes from experiments on reaching in the newborn period. The newborn's ability to reach was a subject of controversy following the initial publication of positive results by Bower, Broughton, and Moore (1970b). However, there are now enough positive replications around for the presence of the ability to be beyond doubt. One of the most interesting of these was carried out by Scania de Schonen (1980). She studied the reaching of infants aged three, four, five, and six days. In full-term infants of five and six days, born without anaesthesia, reaching was observed. It was not observed in three- or four-day-old subjects. In other words, it appeared that four days experience in the world was necessary for this primitive visual-motor-coordination to appear.

I say "experience" rather than postnatal maturation because of some results obtained by Aitken (1981) with premature infants. Every one of these premature babies, all tested before they had reached full term, could reach at least as successfully as term infants of seven days of age. It appears then, that after birth the infant elaborates the visual-motor-coordination we call reaching and that this elaboration depends on experience. Is the coordination truly visual-motor, implying an elaboration from a specific sensory base, or is it perceptual-motor, implying that the base is the higher-order modality-free form of stimulation? One way to test this is to look at the infant's behavior with a completely novel sensory input that retains the form of the information given by vision. This is what we did, using the sonic guide described above (Aitken, 1981; Aitken and Bower, 1981b). The infants were all in the second week of life, and thus had the requisite experience for reaching to seen objects. How would they do with the novel sensory input but perceptually familiar information provided by the guide? They did extremely well, performing in the dark with the sonic guide, even *better* than with vision in light. To ensure that neither result stemmed from simple excitement, we ran another study with another stimulus, in this case a sound-emitting object presented in darkness. This sound-emitting unseen toy could not, as the other two conditions could, give information about distance. On an excitement hypothesis this should not matter. However, as Table 2-1 shows, distance and availability of even novel sensory information about distance were important. The information was used where it was available, as it was with the sonic guide.

It seems to me that the successful transfer of an elaborated perceptual-motor-coordination to a completely new sensory input system is clear evidence that the elaboration was not based on specific sensory inputs but on the formal, perceptual properties of stimulation.

In a previous publication (Bower, 1978), I wrote that the strongest contrary evidence to the view I have been outlining here, was provided by two of its outstanding supporters, Meltzoff and Moore (1977, 1983) who have shown that newborn infants, those whose age can be measured in hours or even minutes, can in fact imitate facial expressions. Imitation, it seemed to me, required a degree of sensory specificity. I would now incline to the view that perhaps it does not. Perhaps, for example, the opening mouth of another is perceived directly as an act of mouth opening, just as is the opening mouth of the baby himself. The input from the outside world maps into the same perceptual structures as the input from the baby's own muscles. If they have the same form — and why should they not? — newborn imitation would be an example of what Michotte (1962b) has called "emphathetic perception," an example of the pickup of formal, perceptual information in the context of the social world rather than of the physical world.

Let me elaborate slightly. What can be happening in imitation? The newborn is presented with a face, part of which moves. Does the newborn see the face or the movement? I am arguing that the newborn sees the movement. Movement is an intermodal variable. The baby can *see* the movement of another and *feel* the movements

Table 2-1 Reaching under three conditions

Condition	Number of reaches	Number of controls	Success (%)
In light	190	110	58
Sound in darkness	200	90	45
Sonic guide in darkness	161	131	81

Source: Aitken, 1981.

31

of his own face. On this view, imitation is simply the intermodal mapping of movement. If this view is correct, one should be able to elicit imitation by presenting pure movement. How to do this? We have used a technique derived from Johanssen (1973) that reduced a face to a pattern of spots of light. As Figure 2-14 shows, the dots are meaningless to us, and to babies. But when the dots move, the gestures are easily seen by adults and newborns. The gestures we have used are eye opening and closing, mouth opening and closing, and mouth protrusion. Babies in the newborn period can imitate films of this kind. The youngest baby I have thus far tested with this kind of presentation was three days old. There was no difference between his imitation of such dot patterns, and his imitation of his mother's face. He imitated both with equal fluency, surely evidence that the higher-order intermodal information that specifies movement is the basis for imitation (Kujawski and Bower, 1985). I emphasize that this is pilot work only, but it does point in the same direction as other work.

The next example of intermodal perception is perhaps different from the last one, or from most of the others I have mentioned, in that, viewed as a skill, it is one in which babies far surpass us adults.

Some years ago Lewis and Brooks (1975) showed that twelve-month-olds can identify the gender of other infants from slides. If shown a slide of a boy side by side with a slide of a girl, boys will look more at the slide of a boy, and girls more at the slide of a girl. There is thus not only differentiation but also "like me" identification. What are the bases of these important social perceptions? The most obvious seemed to be those that are under cultural control: hair length, style and coloring of clothing, and perhaps the associated toys. There have been some studies indicating that these variables are important (Aitken, 1977). Aitken, for example, dressed up boy models in frilly dresses and photographed them holding a doll; his girl models were dressed in dark-colored dungarees and were in the act of banging a drum (Figure 2-15). When showed pairs of slides like this, boys looked more at the girls dressed as boys, and girls more at the boys dressed as girls. In other words, gender identification seemed to be based on low-order, culturally based, empirical cues. A rather different picture emerged when movies were substituted for slides. Here boys looked more at boys, even though dressed as girls, and girls looked more at the girls dressed as boys. It thus

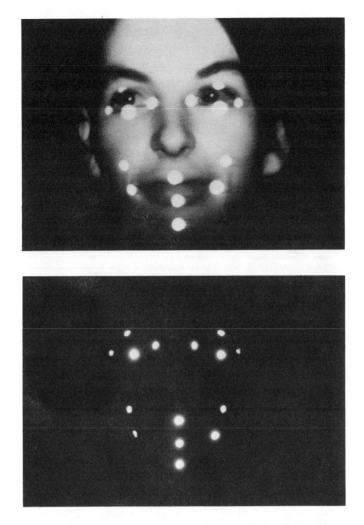

Figure 2-14 A face reduced to a pattern of spots of light. Only when motion is introduced can the dots of light be perceived by both adults and newborns as facial gestures.

appeared that the patterning of movement could be more significant than the low-order cues above.

The next stage in the research was to look at the effect of movement pattern per se, with all other cues to gender, or even "humanness" removed. This was done by using the techniques of Johanssen (1973), mentioned above. A light was attached to the joints of a baby,

A

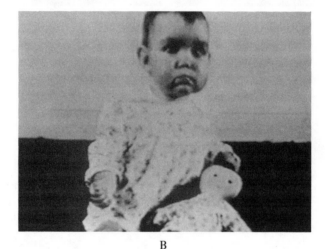

B

Figure 2-15 The gender-appropriate clothes and toys used in Aitken's (1977) experiment. (A) A girl in dungarees with a drum. (B) A boy in a dress with a doll.

one at each shoulder, elbow, wrist, hip, knee, and ankle joint. With the appropriate film technique, nothing is visible in the developed print except these twelve lights. In a still frame the result is not recognizable as a human, much less as a male or female baby (Figure 2-16). Nevertheless, when the films were set in motion, babies had little trouble in identifying the gender of the babies who had modeled the display; twelve-month-old boy babies looked more at the pattern

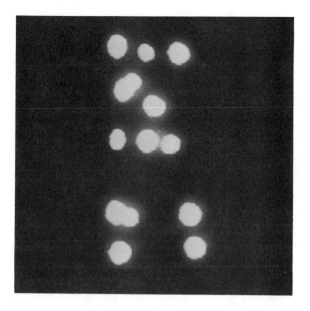

Figure 2-16   Still frame from a film of infant movement, using Johanssen's (1973) technique of attaching lights to 12 joints. (Photograph by Jacqueline Kujawski.)

generated by a baby boy, girl babies more at the pattern generated by a baby girl (Table 2-2). These patterns, in sensory terms, are completely abstract, completely novel to the baby, and yet they yield even better discrimination of gender than a full-color film (Table 2-2). Thus, even at twelve months, perceptual identifications are still

Table 2-2 Duration of first look to paired same-sex and opposite-sex in patch-light and full-color displays

	Same sex	Opposite sex
Patch-light display		
Boy	4.14	2.75
Girl	7.25	1.7
Full-color display		
Boy	4.4	2.9
Girl	5.1	3.5

Source: Kujawski, 1985.

elaborated on the basis of the higher-order, formal properties of stimulation, rather than on the simple, sensory qualities that might seem more obvious. The subjects in this experiment had never before seen a display like the one used, if we define "display" in terms of a simple, sensory quality.

We can also now offer a definition of what constitutes the perceptual world of the newborn, what stimuli from the world of physics and anatomy will be registered in the psychological world of the newborn. I would propose that those events that *can* be specified in a form common to two or more modalities will be registered as events in the psychological world of the newborn. The application of this principle to physical stimuli is obvious. More intriguing, I think, it explains the high degree of interest the baby takes in the stimuli coming from people. The baby has been rehearsing a wide variety of movements, including facial movements, from well before birth. Suddenly there is an external match for these internally known stimuli. If familiarity is important, then newborns have far more familiarity with the information generated by their own movements than they could have with any other type of stimulus. In all probability the most familiar stimuli are those that specify changes in the face, and we know how interested in faces are newborns (e.g., Jirari, 1970).

Perception of course will develop from this starting point, and development from such a starting point can only be a process of differentiations and specification. A very large part of this will be accounted for by restricting the range of possible stimuli the baby is prepared to respond to. Thirty years after the widespread popularization of information theory, many psychologists find it strange still that *potential* stimuli are a major component of information load. The newborn must be preset for many stimuli that he will never actually encounter. As the presentation set is defined in experience, there will be more information processing space freed for analysis of the stimuli that actually occur. No change within the baby is actually required (Bower, 1974, 1982). However, in addition, there will be changes in the baby, actual growth that will permit differentiation, although its role is, I feel, minor. Thus the eye will grow bigger, increasing resolution; the ears will grow further apart, improving auditory localization; and so on. No processes beyond these changes are at all necessary to account for any perceptual changes that may occur after birth.

36

I will expand slightly on these points. It is well known that the identifiability of a stimulus is not simply a function of the presentation characteristics of the stimulus and the receiver characteristics of the organism at the moment of stimulation; the number of possible stimuli — the stimuli that might occur — is a major determinant of performance in such tasks. (e.g., Attneave, 1959) The newborn human is set to expect a much wider range of possible inputs than is the older human. It is this openness that makes possible the intersensory substitution described above, this openness that lets the baby react to humans of all kinds, speaking any known language. Since the presentation set, the set of possible stimuli that might occur, is so large in the world of the newborn, there must be corresponding limits on the detail that is processed. With experience — or lack of experience — some items will fall out of the possible presentation set, reducing its number, and thereby increasing the possibility of detailed processing of the stimulus that actually occurs. This would not require any change or growth within the organism, but would produce effects like those that could be produced by growth. This kind of change will also produce loss. Information-bearing stimuli that are not part of the baby's presentation set will transmit no information. The clearest instances I have seen of this kind of process have been with the sonic guide (see above, p. 26). The ultrasonic echoes produced by all objects are transduced by machine into patterns of sounds. These patterns can convey a great deal of spatial information. However, to older babies they do not; sound as a medium of information is no longer in their presentation set; the presentation set admits sound only as a property of objects. Hence the baby of twenty-five months, presented with a toy in the field of view, of the guide, hearing the sound produced by the guide as it picks up the echo from the toy, takes the toy out of the field of the guide — so there is no more echo — and puts it to her ear, then throws it away in disgust as the sound suddenly disappears.

The world of the newborn has been described in a memorable phrase as a blooming, buzzing confusion. If my speculations have any validity, it is far from that. My newborn's perceptual world is form without content, a structure of places and events, without the rich sensory bloom that so characterizes our own perceptual world. The nearest we can get to understanding the newborn's world is to subject ourselves to a classic experiment on intermodal perception (Figure 2-17). In that experiment there are three sensory events: a flash

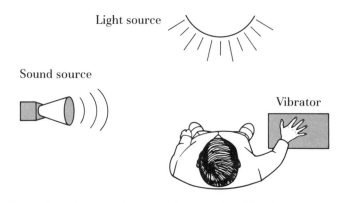

Figure 2-17 Experiment on intermodal perception. The three sensory events, each in a different place, are perceived as movement between three locations.

of light, a single sound, and touch, each in a different place. What we adults perceive is movement between three locations; we do not see the movement, we do not hear the movement nor do we feel it. We perceive it, an experience as close to pure perception as we adults can attain, an experience, I would say, like those of the newborn child.

To close this chapter, I would like to argue that perception as we have described it would produce some long-term effects in development, in conjunction with a very simple learning and remembering system. Perception in the young infant is more general than that of an adult. The infant, in this view, would not remember a social encounter with a blue-eyed woman as "the blue-eyed woman did . . ." but as "people *do* . . ." or "women do . . . ." As Fodor (1980) among others has argued, the infant perceives general truths, "general" and "true" in the mind of the baby. This kind of process could lead to long-term effects. Consider the following not wholly imaginary scenario. A woman wearing long dangly earrings picks up and plays with a baby. The baby seizes an earring and pulls. The woman screams and drops the baby. This event would instantiate the general premise that all women wearing earrings are unreliable.

Part of the thrust of the previous analysis has been to support the idea that the infant will act in terms of these general ideas or representations or percepts. The premise outlined above would lead to suspicious behavior in the infant, behavior to which adult females would be susceptible (Stott, 1959), eliciting behavior in them that could confirm the original hypothesis. A male infant who has had this kind of experience might reach adulthood incapable of a meaningful relationship with any woman who wore earrings. This would be an instance of far transfer indeed, transfer mediated by a premise instantiated in infancy, a premise that would lead to behavior that would render the premise incontrovertible.

This instance is deliberately fanciful. I am sure that any one of us could work out model processes for more realistic long-term effects. They would depend on no more than the baby's propensity to perceive in general terms and a propensity to act in terms of what is perceived. The resulting behaviors could reinforce and sustain the initial representation.

Learning

In the two previous chapters the term *learning* has been used in a casual, common-sense way. In this chapter I would like to specify what learning means to me. I think that my ideas are quite conventional, so conventional that in my previous writing and teaching I have assumed that no exposition was required. I have recently become aware that the teaching of American behavior theory is no longer as universal as it was in my youth, so that I am all too often at cross-purposes with my audience. It is to avoid this that I am imposing this brief review on you.

The study of learning by psychologists has been an American preoccupation. It is American psychologists who have forged the theories of learning that in some form are *the* theory in psychology. I personally know scarcely any psychologists who do not operate, implicitly or explicitly, with some version of American learning theory as their basic explanatory paradigm. Even such a fabulous original as Jean Piaget felt compelled to outline how he differed from American learning theorists as a way of explaining what he was actually proposing (see e.g., Piaget, *The Psychology of Intelligence*, 1942b, 1951). In a different way, even the would-be revolutionary R. D. Laing, proposing an existential psychiatry in *Self and Others* (1967) at base relies on American learning theory for his fundamental explanatory paradigms (see Bower, 1979).

At one time it must have seemed that there was no such thing as American behavior theory; the welkin rang the sounds of battle between different theorists who maintained different theories, in violent opposition, or so it seemed. From an outside perspective these differences seem very minor. Writing as a non-American, albeit American trained, I feel that I can describe American behavior theory or learning theory without doing violence to any of those who fought so long.

What then are the key tenets of learning theory? As I see it, the basic form of all learning is *association* or *connection* between events that were not associated or connected prior to learning. In the earliest learning theory, that of Thorndike *Animal Intelligence*, (1898), learning was the "association between sense impressions and impulses to action," between the effects of stimuli from the world and acts performed on and in the world. "The effects of stimuli" is often shortened to "S" and "acts performed on and in the world" are often called responses or "R." Thorndike's psychology is thus the original S-R psychology. S-R associations were not the only linkages of interest. Tolman (1932) and his numerous coworkers were much more interested in linkages between stimuli, S-S learning. Lastly, with Skinner (e.g., 1953) the focus is on the association between an act and its consequences; to fit in with the preceding system of labels this would have to be called R-S learning, although Skinner would doubtless object, and rightly so.

All of the theories are about what goes with what, whether it is stimulus with stimulus, response with response, or any combination. The subject of learning theory is the detection of relations between events. The detection of relationships of course depends on the prior detection of the events. The terminology I am using would not amuse any of the theorists I have mentioned. However, I am unashamed, since my aim is to give a simple description of what they have been about, rather than a summary of what they said they were about.

Given that the basic focus of learning theory is association, the major controversies were over how the associations were formed and how we could ever know that they had been formed. The simplest answer to the first question (along with an implicit answer to the second) was that given by Guthrie (1935). "A combination of stimuli which has accompanied a movement will on its recurrence tend to be followed by that movement." In other words, every co-occurrence of events can produce an association between the events; in the case of S-R association we can tell that the association has been formed because R will be more likely to occur, given S. While simple, Guthrie's model is powerful; it provided the core of the mathematical learning theories that tortured my own student days. Its essential statement is that any pair of events that "co-occur" (occur at the same time) can be associated, and that by looking at response rates or response probabilities *we* as experimenters can know whether or not the association has been formed.

Guthrie, like every other theorist, thought that *reinforcement* is important in learning. Another way to put it would be to say that he believed that "reward" was important in learning. The precise role assigned to reinforcement varied among theorists. All theorists believed that an act performed in a certain stimulus context was most likely to recur if it was followed by some rewarding consequence. Some argued that only those associations that were themselves associated with a pleasant consequence would be learned. Others argued that all associations were learned but only those with pleasant consequences would be utilized and their occurrence therefore measured. All agreed that reinforcement was important for performance, and that the measurement of performance was the only way to measure learning.

The definition of the word "reinforcement" has varied from theorist to theorist. Some have restricted reinforcement to biological necessities, such as food and water; others have included anything pleasant. The most neutral definition would seem to be that offered by Skinner: a positive reinforcer is anything that increases the probability of a preceding, associated response. Please note that once again an increase in rate of response is the favored measure. Skinner discovered that different schedules of reinforcement could have different effects on the increases in rate. His description of the effects of different schedules defines a set of "facts," "true" statements in every theory thus discussed. In all theories, if only for the sake of getting performance measures, experiments are designed so that acts produce reinforcing consequences. We can — and everyone before Skinner did — set up the experiment so that every occurrence of the act produces a reinforcement. This is referred to as *continuous reinforcement* (CRF).

Thus suppose we have a pigeon in the famous Skinner box. In the box there is a key. On CRF every peck at the key would result in the delivery of reinforcement, typically food. The rate of key pecking is increased by the association of key pecking with the delivery of food. In the real world, CRF is supposedly rare. Skinner therefore introduced various schedules of *intermittent* or *partial reinforcement*. A simple intermittent schedule is the *fixed ratio* (FR) schedule. In an FR schedule every x^{th} response is reinforced; x could be 5 so that the organism would have to respond five times to obtain one reinforcement. Our pigeon in the Skinner box on such a schedule — an FR_5 schedule — would have to peck five times to obtain one delivery of food. The ratio can be set at any number the experimenter wishes, FR_4, FR_{15}, FR_{200}, or whatever. Fixed ratio schedules produce higher rates of responding than CRF. In general the higher the ratio the higher the rate of response: the less frequent is the reinforcement, the more rapid is the response. With high ratios there tends to be a pause after each reinforcement.

The *variable ratio* (VR) *schedule* introduces more uncertainty into the situation. In a VR schedule the experimenter decides what number of responses, *on average*, is required for a reinforcement; however the actual number required varies from reinforcement to reinforcement. Thus on a VR_6 schedule the bird might receive food after 4 responses; then on such a schedule may receive food after 8, 2, 10, 7, 5, 2, 4, 12 responses, successively. The average ratio of responses to reinforcements is $6:1$, but the precise number required varies around the mean of 6 to yield a VR_6 schedule. Variable ratio schedules produce higher rates than the corresponding FR schedules. Even with high ratios there is no pause in response after reinforcement.

Corresponding to the ratio schedules there are two varieties of interval schedule. On an interval schedule, reinforcement is available only after a period of time after the preceding reinforcement. With a *fixed interval* (FI) *schedule* of 30 seconds. FI_{30}, no response will produce reinforcement until 30 seconds after the last reinforcement. After the 30 seconds has passed the first response will produce the reinforcement. With a *variable interval* (VI) *schedule*, the average interval between reinforcements is fixed; however the effective interval varies about that average, changing from reinforcement to reinforcement. These schedules do not produce such high rates as the ratio schedules, the rate of response actually declining somewhat as the interval increases. A characteristic scalloping is seen with FI schedules, the bulk of responding occurring just prior to the end of the interval (Figure 3-1). The scalloping is abolished with VI schedules.

The interval and ratio schedules are the best known and best studied of the modifications introduced by Skinner. However, there is one other, which is of burgeoning theoretical interest, the modification he called accidental contingency but which we shall refer to as noncontingent reinforcement (NCR), which is delivered on some predetermined schedule that is independent of the animal's behavior. In the standard Skinner box, food is delivered whatever the bird is doing. Skinner showed with pigeons that noncontingent reinforcement could produce "superstitious" behavior. The birds tended to repeat whatever they had been doing just prior to the delivery of food

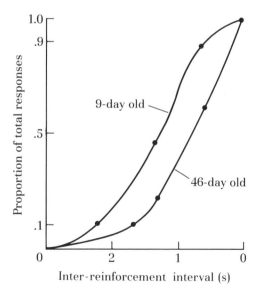

Figure 3-1 The scalloping effect observed with fixed interval schedules.

although that behavior had no contingent relationship to food delivery *in fact*; but clearly it did in the mind of the pigeon.

Thus far we have looked at the acquisition of associations, the process whereby one event comes to elicit or signal another. Of equal importance is the opposite process in which such associations are *unlearned*. This latter process is referred to as extinction. It seems that extinction is not a spontaneous process resulting from lack of use of a learned association. Pigeons removed from a Skinner box for four years showed the appropriate key-pecking immediately on reintroduction (Skinner, 1950). If we wish to extinguish an association, we must take steps rather than relying on the effect of time. It would seem plausible to characterize learning as the detection of a contingent relation between two events, so that the occurrence of the first causes or signals the onset of the other. Surely extinction should occur if we simply present the first event without the second event.

Suppose we consider a type of learning we have not looked at before — *classical conditioning*. In classical conditioning, discovered by Pavlov (1950) the experimenter controls two events. One of these is referred to as the *unconditioned stimulus* (UCS). The characteristic of the UCS is that by itself it will produce some automatic response from the organism, *unconditioned response* (UCR). Pavlov's favorite UCS was food, presented to a hungry animal. This UCS produces a flow of saliva from the animal. Various other UCS have been used, such as a puff of air on the eyeball, spontaneously eliciting a blink. The *conditioned stimulus* (CS) is any other stimulus that does not elicit that UCR. Suppose then we have a hungry dog. We ring a bell, then we present food. The dog will salivate at the sight and smell of the food. After a few pairings the dog will begin to salivate at the sound of the bell. In this situation the CS in the bell, the UCS the food, and salivation to food the UCR. The salivation that comes to be elicited by the bell is referred to as the *conditioned response* (CR).

Suppose we carry out conditioning until the CS reliably produces a CR. What will happen if we omit the UCS? In time the conditioned response to the conditioned stimulus will be extinguished. The CS, the bell, will sound and no salivation will occur. So far so simple! The dog learned that the bell signaled food and then learned that the bell no longer signaled food. No problem yet. The first problem that crops up is the phenomenon of *spontaneous recovery*. If we thoroughly extinguish a CS-CR link, like the one described above, so that the CS elicits no CR, and then rest our organism for a while, the next presentation of the CS will elicit a CR. This is the phenomenon referred to as spontaneous recovery. It seems to be characteristic of all forms of learning.

Numerous theorists come up with the same explanation of spontaneous recovery and with a new theory of how to extinguish learned associations. I will refer to this theory of extinction as "interference theory." In essence this latter theory argues that the procedure described in the last paragraph could not produce true extinction because the procedure taught the animal nothing new. Initially the animal was taught that a CS, a bell, would be followed by a UCS, food. Afterwards food was omitted. An animal, the theory proposes, cannot learn an association between something and nothing, so the original association between something and something, a bell and food, will remain intact.

The disappearance of the CR in the extinction procedure outlined above is no more than fatigue, or so says the interference theory; given rest, the learned association will of course reappear. To obtain true extinction it is necessary to replace the original learning so that the original CS elicits a different CR, a CR incompatible with the original. In one classic study (Kellog and Walks, 1938) dogs were presented with a buzzer as CS followed by an electric shock to the right paw. The CR was lifting of the right paw. In the extinction phase, the same buzzer was the conditioned stimulus but the shock was delivered to the left paw. In this situation, extinction of right-foot-lifting was seen although as many as 100 trials were necessary for the extinction to occur.

There is one other complication to extinction that I must mention; that is the complication introduced by what is called *generalization*. Suppose we teach an animal that a particular stimulus is the signal for a particular response. Different stimuli will elicit the same response. These are referred to as generalization stimuli. We can say (although we will have to qualify this later) that the more like the original stimulus the new stimulus is, the more likely is the new stimulus to elicit a conditioned response. There is also generalization of extinction. However, the generalization of extinction does not follow the same stimulus similarity rules as generalization of acquisition. Thus it can happen that extinction of response to the original stimulus is complete but new, generalization stimuli can still elicit the conditioned response at a high level (e.g., Perkins and Weyant, 1958). Indeed it can happen that a generalization stimulus will elicit

47

far more responses than the original reinforced stimulus (Guttman and Kalish, 1958). The simple aim, to accomplish unlearning, becomes very complicated in the light of such findings. These paradoxes can be explained by recourse to slightly unusual ideas about stimulus similarity, ideas akin to those outlined in the last chapter. We will put them aside for the moment.

Extinction is also affected by the nature of the association that has been formed. For example it is usually very difficult to accomplish the extinction of learned avoidance behavior. In learned avoidance behavior there is an unconditioned stimulus that is unpleasant. A conditioned stimulus is introduced as a signal for the occurrence of the unconditioned stimulus. The animal can take steps to avoid the infliction of the UCS. Thus if the UCS is an electric shock in one part of the floor, the animal can learn to avoid that part, moving away from it on presentation of the CS. Clearly under normal circumstances the animal will never learn that the UCS is no longer being delivered, since the conditioned response ensures that the animal has moved away from its place of delivery. Extinction in this kind of situation can be facilitated if the animal is forced to stay where the shock had been delivered, that is, forcibly prevented from performing the CR. Under these circumstances the animal can learn that the CS no longer signals the UCS; under these circumstances the CR will no longer occur. However, animals who have undergone such extinction may show no more conditioned responses, but the conditioned stimulus will elicit in them even more fear (measured in other ways) than it will in animals who have not undergone extinction of the CS-CR link (Page, 1955). Once again it is clear that extinction is a complicated process, difficult to accomplish in any straightforward way.

While I have emphasized that learning and extinction are complicated, I do feel that existing theory can account for them and their paradoxes, particularly if it incorporates some of the ideas about perception that were described in the last chapter. Let us agree that learning involves the detection of a relationship between two events, so that the organism that has learned believes that the occurrence of the first event is a reliable signal for the occurrence of the second; if we are so inclined, we can say that our organism believes that there is a contingent relation between the first event and the second event, and thus that learning is the detection of contingencies. If we, or the world, present an organism with a contingent relation, the organism may or may not detect it. Clearly the organism can only detect a relationship between events if the organism can perceive the events. Furthermore the relation that is detected will be determined by the way the organism perceives the events. The organism's perception of the events may well be different from our own; it is nothing but monstrous egocentrism to assume otherwise.

For example, a fair proportion of the human male population has trouble discriminating colors. I am one of them. If I were placed in a situation in which the experimenter had set things up so that a flash of red light signaled a shock to the right hand and a flash of blue light signaled a shock to the left hand, the contingency I would detect would be "a flash of colored light signals an impending shock to one hand or the other."

We can make sense of many seeming anomalies in learning by remembering that what has been learned may not be what we were trying to teach; in our present context, the developing child, we must remember that the perceptual system changes, so that what has been learned may be beyond the reach of correction or extinction. I can give an example by referring you to the deservedly famous case of "Little Albert" (Watson and Rayner, 1920), a case we soon will discuss in detail (pp. 50–53).

The above comments on perception and learning are obviously true, I think, as well as truly obvious. The same ideas have been extended with profit to the circumstances and schedules of learning The terminology I find most useful here is that of Krechevsky (1932, 1938). "Learning . . . is a . . . process in which the learner theoretically tests and rejects a series of *hypotheses* until the correct one is hit upon." Adding this hypothesis-testing terminology to the formulation used before, we can say that a learning organism is formulating and testing hypotheses about contingent relations between events.

The experimental situation will allow a particular hypothesis to be established. How rapidly that hypothesis can be disestablished or extinguished will be a function of the experimental situation. Clearly an hypothesis formed under partial reinforcement will take longer to extinguish because it will take the organism longer to detect that the circumstances have changed. Avoidance learning will take a long time to extinguish because the animal will never allow itself to discover that the situation has changed. The paradox of extinction of an avoidance response with increased fear of the CS that had elicited it (p. 48) can be looked at in the same way. The animal has learned that the CS signals shock in a particular place. That is one item of learning. The shock can be avoided by leaving that place. That is the second item of learning. When the experimenter restrains the animal in the place, the animal learns that shock can be avoided by doing whatever it was doing while the experimenter restrained it. That is the third item of learning. The third item will interfere with performance of the second item. However, it will in no way affect the first item. Indeed, the first item is an hypothesis that is validated by both the second and the third item, so that the paradox, in Krechevsky's reasoning, is no longer a paradox.

My discussion thus far has woven itself around organisms in general rather than humans, adult or infant. One of the most important experiments in the history of the psychology of learning was carried out on the human infant subject, Albert B. (Watson and Rayner op. cit.).

This infant was reared almost from birth in a hospital environment; his mother was a wet nurse in the Harriet Lane Home for Invalid Children. Albert's life was normal: he was healthy from birth and one of the best developed youngsters ever brought to the hospital, weighing twenty-one pounds at nine months of age. He was on the whole stolid and unemotional. His stability was one of the principal reasons for using him as a subject in this test. We felt that we could do him relatively little harm by carrying out such experiments as those outlined below.

At approximately nine months of age we ran him through the emotional tests that have become a part of our regular routine in determining whether fear reactions can be called out by other stimuli than sharp noises. The infant was confronted suddenly and for the first time successively with a white rat, a rabbit, a dog, a monkey, with masks with and without hair, cotton wool, burning newspapers, etc. *At no time did this infant ever show fear in any situation.*

This happy state was not to continue. Albert, like other infants, was frightened by loud noises. The experimenters arranged to present Albert with a pairing, a possible contingent association, between a neutral stimulus and the unconditioned stimulus for fear, a loud noise, produced by striking a steel bar with a hammer. The dire consequences are well described in the authors' own notes.

11 months, 3 days

1. White rat suddenly taken from the basket and presented to Albert. He began to reach for rat with left hand. Just as his hand touched

the animal the bar was struck immediately behind his head. The infant jumped violently and fell forward, burying his face in the mattress. He did not cry, however.

2. Just as the right hand touched the rat the bar was again struck. Again the infant jumped violently, fell forward and began to whimper. In order not to disturb the child too seriously no further tests were given for one week.

11 months, 10 days

1. Rat presented suddenly without sound. There was steady fixation but no tendency at first to reach for it. The rat was then placed nearer, whereupon tentative reaching movements began with the right hand. When the rat nosed the infant's left hand, the hand was immediately withdrawn. He started to reach for the head of the animal with the forefinger of the left hand, but withdrew it suddenly before contact. It is thus seen that the two joint stimulations given the previous week were not without effect. He was tested with his blocks immediately afterwards to see if they shared in the process of conditioning. He began immediately to pick them up, dropping them, pounding them, etc. In the remainder of the tests the blocks were given frequently to quiet him and to test his general emotional state. They were always removed from sight when the process of conditioning was under way.

2. Joint stimulation with rat and sound. Started, then fell over immediately to right side. No crying.

3. Joint stimulation. Fell to side and rested upon hands, with head turned away from rat. No crying.

4. Joint stimulation. Same reaction.

5. Rat suddenly presented alone. Puckered face, whimpered and withdrew body sharply to the left.

6. Joint stimulation. Fell over immediately to right side and began to whimper.

7. Joint stimulation. Started violently and cried, but did not fall over.

8. Rat alone. *The instant the rat was shown the baby began to cry. Almost instantly he turned sharply to the left, fell over on left side, raised himself on all fours and began to crawl away so rapidly that he was caught with difficulty before reaching the edge of the table.*

51

The authors tested for generalization and found it occurring to a dog, a rabbit, a sealskin coat, cotton wool, Watson's hair but not that of two others, and a Santa Claus mask. Further trials with and without the UCS were given with the rat, the dog, and the rabbit. Thirty-one days after this, Albert was retested. All of the stimuli elicited fear, in particular the fur coat, a stimulus which had never been directly associated with a loud noise (Figure 3-2).

This study shows the rapidity of learning in an infant. It also shows how the infant will learn more than we think he might. Albert has learned to fear hairy things rather than to fear a white rat. Since the fear removes Albert from the stimulus or the stimulus from Albert, there is no reason why the fear response should ever extinguish. It would be a stable developmental effect. Indeed Watson and Rayner assume that they had created a stable developmental effect.

The Freudians twenty years from now, when they come to analyze Albert's fear of a seal skin coat — assuming that he comes to analysis at that age — will probably tease from him the recital of a dream which

Figure 3-2 Little Albert was trained to fear a white rat. He showed fear of all the other things shown which, as sensory stimuli, are very different from a white rat.

upon their analysis will show that Albert at three years of age attempted to play with the pubic hair of the mother and was scolded violently for it. (We are by no means denying that this might in some other case condition it.) If the analyst has sufficiently prepared Albert to accept such a dream when found as an explanation of his avoiding tendencies, and if the analyst has the authority and personality to put it over, Albert may be fully convinced that the dream was a true revealer of the factors which brought out the fear.

It is probable that many of the phobias in psychopathology are true conditioned emotional reactions either of the direct or the transferred type.

It seems unlikely that Albert would ever touch anyone's pubic hair, in fact. This study, reprehensible as it now seems, does show how early experience could have long-term effects. In this case the effects are negative but the same paradigm would handle positive effects, using the simple principles of learning theory.

4

Learning in Infants

The last chapter closed with an account of one of the most famous experiments in the history of the psychology, an experiment that featured an infant. Despite this early start it was a long time before it was generally accepted that infants, particularly young infants, could learn in the full sense of the word. These doubts are now long gone. It is accepted that newborns can learn, and begin learning, immediately. Indeed Lipsitt (1969) could write ". . . with respect to some human attributes the developmental decline or social destruction of a response may begin at birth." By every conventional measure newborn humans are extremely efficient learning machines. Indeed, the conventional measures may underestimate the capacity of our organism.

I have a few reservations about conventional measures of learning.

These few quibbles began with a major query about the nature of reinforcement in infancy. As we saw in the last chapter, every theory of learning assumes that reinforcement is important for learning, for performance, or both. What is reinforcement? Some theories have tried to tie reinforcement to the satisfaction of basic biological needs. The infant human especially has been target for this kind of theorizing. The infant interest in human adults has been explained away as an interest in providers of food and water. Indeed all human motives have been reduced to this base level, with the infant the supposed source of evidence. There is evidence that infants will act to obtain food, sweet tastes, and the like. However, it is very clear that such motives are not the motives for learning in infancy.

It is rare for students of learning in infancy to rely on hunger or food rewards for reinforcement. It is much more common to present an "interesting event" consequent and contingent upon the performance of an act by the baby. The interesting events have ranged from presentation of a whole human being to the momentary illumination of a light bulb. Papousek (1969) pointed out that the reinforcer did not seem important. Paralleling a suggestion by Watson (1972), he suggested that the reward for the baby was the solution of the problem posed in the experiment. Learning, for both of these authors, involved the formulation and testing of hypotheses, reward or reinforcement being in the confirmation of the hypotheses. Both authors have gone on to substantiate these ideas. (e.g., Watson, 1985).

It is at this point that reservations about conventional measures of learning must come forward. Learning has been equated with the increase in rate of a response that has been embedded in a contingent pairing. A pigeon's peck at a key produces food. The pigeon shows us that it has learned the contingency by increasing the rate of key-pecking. That is all well and good for a hungry pigeon, a pigeon that has been starved to 80 percent of its normal body weight. It seems most inappropriate for an infant testing hypotheses.

Let us take seriously the idea that an infant in an operant learning situation is formulating and testing hypotheses. Let us suppose the situation is the commonplace one in which a limb movement by the baby, l, produces one second of movement of a mobile, m. The experimenter has arranged things so that there is a contingent relation between the two events, l and m. How can we know that the baby has detected the contingency? We might look for an increase in rate of responding. However, an increase in rate should not satisfy us any more than it should satisfy the baby, or the baby as described by Watson (op. cit.) and Papousek (op. cit.).

Suppose our baby is lying there making random limb movements. Our baby then notices that the mobile is occasionally turning. He begins to suspect that there is some relationship between limb movement and mobile movement. He begins, In Krechevsky's terms, to formulate a hypothesis about a possible relation between l and m.

This hypothesis would generate behavior to confirm or deny the hypothesis. Krechevsky's rats showed appropriate behavior and we would expect human infants to do so too. Part of the behavior would be an increase in rate. The baby would test and check that the conjunction — limb movement, then mobile movement — actually did occur. We will label that conjunction $l.m$ The symbol "." is a construction for "and." If there is a contingent relation between l and m then the conjunction $l.m$ ought to occur reliably and significantly more than the baby would expect it to occur by chance.

This is where the limitations of rate increase become obvious. If the baby moves his limbs continuously, the mobile will move continuously. What does this tell the baby? Nothing! The only way the baby can ascertain that there is a relation between l and m is by withholding l for part of the time, and looking to see whether or not m ever occurs without a preceding l. For the baby to conclude that there really is a relation between $l.m$, he must be able to calculate that the probability of a mobile movement given a leg movement is greater than the probability of a mobile movement given no leg movement. He must be able to work out that

$$p\,l.m > p{-}l.m,$$

where p = probability, l = limb movement, m = mobile movement, $>$ = greater than, and $-$ = not, so that $-l$ means no limb movement. In the same way I propose that the baby would seek to ascertain that $p{-}l.{-}m > pl.{-}m$, that the probability of no mobile movement given no limb movement is greater than the probability of no mobile movement given limb movement.

We are taught in our elementary texts of statistics that both of these inequalities must hold if we are to assert that there is a contingent relationship between l and m. The behavior we should look for in the learning situation is behavior that would allow the baby to confirm the truth inequalities. This behavior would surely include some high rate activity, but would also include pauses to allow the baby to check what happens with no limb movement. It makes little sense for us to look for rate increase alone; we should be looking for a change in the pattern of activity, a change to a pattern that shows systematic increases in activity *and* systematic pauses in activity.

Figure 4-1 shows an experimental arrangement which allowed just such a contingency to be introduced into the environment of an eight-week-old baby. The baby is reclining with support before a translucent screen. Behind the screen is a projector. Between the projector and the screen is a mobile decorated with colored translucent pieces of plastic. The projector produces an image of the mobile on the screen, where it is visible to the baby. A light source on the baby's left illuminates a photocell on the baby's right. A leg movement by the baby will cut the photocell beam. This interruption is registered by a microcomputer. The microcomputer records all leg movements with their time of occurrence and computes inter-response intervals. The computer controls the movement of the mobile. In this and later studies, continuous reinforcement (CRF) means that every time the light beam is broken the computer switches on the mobile motor for one second. The motor is then switched off until the next interruption occurs.

Figure 4-2 shows what happened when CRF was introduced after a period with no mobile movement at all. As can be seen there, there was a pronounced change in the pattern of responding, a change of the kind proposed above. In principle one could work out the period of inaction that the baby uses as a basis for $-l$ calculations from data of the sort given there. Let us leave that aside for the moment. Instead let us review the claims that we have made about the learning that is going on in this simple operant situation. We have proposed that the baby formulates the hypothesis that there is a contingent relation between this leg movement and the movement of the mobile. He tests this hypothesis by behaving so as to obtain information that will allow him to assert the truth of the two inequalities

$$pl.m > p{-}l.m \quad \text{and} \quad p{-}l.{-}m > pl.{-}m$$

As we have seen, the baby does behave in a way that fits this line of thought. Is there anything more we could do to make sure that the baby

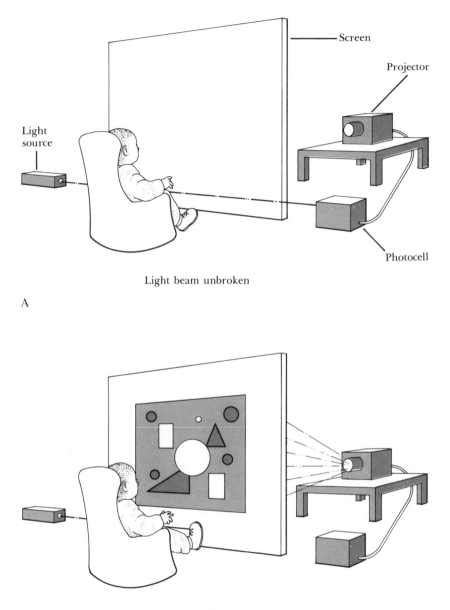

Light beam unbroken

A

Light beam blocked by baby's boot

B

Figure 4-1

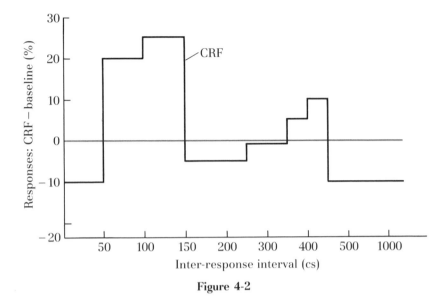

Figure 4-2

is learning, has learned? The two inequalities displayed above give us a way. Each is a statement about the causal texture of the environment the baby finds himself in. Each, in a situation with continuous reinforcement, takes on extreme values. Thus, in CRF, the probability of mobile movement, given a leg movement, $p\,l.m$, is 1.0; that is, it always happens. The probability of mobile movement, given no leg movement, $p-l.m$, is zero; it never happens. These are facts of the experimental situation. If the baby has learned these facts, he should be surprised if we change them, as we could by introducing an instance of noncontingent reinforcement, an instance where the mobile moves without a preceding leg movement, an instance of $-l.m$.

We could reasonably do the same with the other inequality. In CRF the probability of no mobile movement, given no leg movement, $p-l.-m$, is 1.0; the probability of no mobile movement, given a limb movement, $p\,l.-m$, is zero. Here we could introduce an instance of partial reinforcement, an instance of $l.-m$, to see whether the baby is surprised. Surprise would indicate that the baby had concrete expectations in the situation, expectations that had been violated by the new event-pairing.

Table 4-1 shows the results of such manipulations. Two groups of six-to-eight-week-old babies were introduced to the operant situation described above. The schedule gave CRF. After eight reinforcements

Table 4-1 Change in responding of two groups of infants (6 to 8 weeks old) introduced to the operant mobile situation

Group	NCR	No reinforcement
1	1.33	
2		.86

Note: The figures were obtained by dividing the mean inter-response interval before the novel event by the mean inter-response interval for the first three responses after the novel event

Source: Petrie, Symonds, and Bower (in prep).

had been delivered either noncontingent reinforcement was delivered, mobile movement with no preceding limb movement, $-l.m$, or the ninth leg movement did not produce mobile movement, an instance of $l.-m$. Both innovations produced large changes in rate, evidence of surprise and hence of learning.

A careful inspection of Figures 4-2 and 4-3 may puzzle the attentive reader. The changes are there and very plain to see, but the nature of the changes is surely not that predicted by behavior theory. Just what predictions would behavior theory make? What should happen to behavior as a consequence of the manipulations we have introduced? I propose to present two sets of possible predictions,

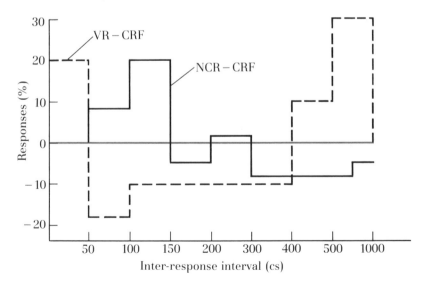

Figure 4-3

both derived from the same body of theory. In fact the first predictions derive from an unreflective reading of behavior theory.

Consider the effect of withholding reinforcement. This changes the schedule from continuous reinforcement to partial reinforcement — as we have all known since Skinner's response rate increase under partial reinforcement. But wait a minute! We know that Skinner's result is true beyond doubt in the experimental situations he used. We can also see that in the situation we are discussing, the baby and the mobile, the very opposite pattern ensues, with the rate actually dropping. But why should we expect the behavior pattern that holds for a hungry pigeon to hold for an unstressed infant, interested only in the problem of the situation?

The other manipulation, noncontingent reinforcement (NCR), also produces results opposite to those we might expect from a straightforward reading of behavior theory. As the term implies, a noncontingent reinforcement is delivered only after a period in which the operant response has not occurred. We can be certain that the baby was doing something in this time period, that some act would occur just prior to the delivery of reinforcement. That act, surely would thus become more probable and would thus interfere with the execution of the operant response, resulting in a decline in the rate of the operant response. As Figure 4-3 shows, noncontingent reinforcement actually produces an increase in the response rate of the babies in the situation we are discussing.

Why should this be? To understand what is going on, we have to return to Krechevsky and simplify his ideas to some extent. Krechevsky, remember, proposed that learning is the formulation and testing of hypotheses, with incoming information used only to evaluate the hypotheses under test. Our baby, in a situation where leg movement produces mobile movement, is given good solid information that there is some relationship between his leg movements and mobile movements. We can be sure that the baby will try to work out the precise nature of that relationship. Unfortunately the situation does not present the baby with enough information to specify the relationship. This may surprise you. To explain what I mean I will have to introduce some simple ideas derived from logic.

In the operant situation described, the baby might formulate the hypothesis, "whenever my leg moves, the mobile moves." This sentence, written using the logical symbol "→", becomes "my leg moves

→ the mobile moves" (the arrow symbolizes the "whenever" relationship). The baby's hypothesis can thus be written

$$l \rightarrow m$$

While $l \rightarrow m$ looks forbidingly logical, it is only a shorthand way of writing "whenever my leg moves, the mobile moves." Logic offers a system of rules for deciding when hypotheses of this sort are valid and when they are invalid. Hypotheses of this kind describe a relation between two events. On some pairings of events the hypothesis is true or valid; on others it is false or invalid. What are the possible pairings of events here? There are two events and each either happens or it does not. The possible pairings are

my leg moves	the mobile moves
my leg does not move	the mobile moves
my leg moves	the mobile does not move
my leg does not move	the mobile does not move

If we again use l and m, and the symbol $-$ to mean "not," we can write the above pairings as follows:

$$
\begin{array}{cc}
l & m \\
-l & m \\
l & -m \\
-l & -m
\end{array}
$$

We can now see that there are four possible pairings of events: $l.m$, $-l.m$, $l.-m$, and $-l.-m$, where the symbol "." between letters means "and." With that information we can rewrite yet another version of these event pairings.

The hypothesis we are examining, $l \rightarrow m$, "whenever my leg moves, the mobile moves," has two components, "my leg moves" and "the mobile moves." Each of these events either occurs or it does not. The components are thus either true (t) or false (f), true if the event occurs as stated, false if it does not. We can thus state the following:

my leg moves (*l*)	the mobile moves (*m*)
t	t
f	t
t	f
f	f

This is an example of a "truth" table. It contains the truth values for the components of the hypothesis under test. With a truth table, one can use a simple algorithm to decide when an hypothesis about the relation between two events is true and when it is false.

The algorithm depends on an assumption about value. It is assumed that "true" is the highest truth value and "false" the lowest truth value. Thus the value of a false statement is by definition lower than the value of a true statement. Suppose now we have an hypothesis about the relation between two events, like the one we are considering, $l \rightarrow m$. That hypothesis is true or valid if the value of the component on the left of the logical symbol, "$\rightarrow$", is less than or equal to the value of the component on the right of the symbol. The hypothesis is false or invalid if the value of the component on the left is greater than the value of the component on the right. We can thus evaluate our hypothesis as

l	*m*	$l \rightarrow m$
t	t	t
f	t	t
t	f	f
f	f	t

The pairing of events on the third line, "my leg moves and the mobile does not move" would falsify the hypothesis because *l* would have a higher value than *m*. On the other three pairings the hypothesis is true. The hypothesis the baby might adopt thus predicts that three conjunctions of events will occur and one will not.

This hypothesis about the relationship between leg movement and mobile movement thus predicts that the three compound events, $l.m$, $-l.-m$, and $-l.m$ (leg movement and mobile movement; no leg movement and no mobile movement; and no leg movement and mobile movement), will occur, and that one compound, $l.-m$ (leg movement and no mobile movement), will not. Again, using the symbols "$-$" = not, "$.$" = and, and "$\vee$" = or, the hypothesis predicts

$$(l.m \vee -l.-m \vee -l.m).-(l.-m)$$

The above is no more than a complete logical definition of the hypothesis, $l \rightarrow m$.

At this point, I should take some time to explain how I am using the word "hypothesis," and the relation between the hypothesis and the logical structure. The word "hypothesis" is frequently used to explain what goes on in perception, a usage common from Helmholtz to the present day. As such, it clearly has no implication of conscious ratiocination. In an operant conditioning situation with CRF, the organism is presented with information from the outside world, just as in perception. The structure that detects information must be susceptible to formal description. I am proposing that the symbol "$\rightarrow$" is a description of the structure that detects operant contingencies.

It is worth sticking with the perception analogy for the moment. The information given to an organism by CRF is inherently ambiguous. The baby in our situation is given only two conjunctions, $l.m$ and $-l.-m$. These are consonant with the hypothesis $l \rightarrow m$. However they are also consonant with another hypothesis, the hypothesis $-l \rightarrow -m$, "if my leg does not move, the mobile will not move." The full definition of $-l \rightarrow -m$ is

l	m	$-l$	$-m$	$-l \rightarrow -m$
t	t	f	f	t
f	t	t	f	f
t	f	f	t	t
f	f	t	t	t

It is worth noting that, given that $l.m$ and $-l.m$ do occur, there are only two hypotheses consonant with the information given, $l{\rightarrow}m$ or $-l{\rightarrow}-m$, and the information given is ambiguous about which is correct, which one is true.

The initial ambiguity of CRF can be resolved by more information, specifically by an instance of $-l.m$ or of $l.-m$. An instance of $-l.m$ would instantly define $-l{\rightarrow}-m$ as false and $l{\rightarrow}m$ as true. An instance of $l.-m$ would likewise inform the organism that $l{\rightarrow}m$ is false and $-l{\rightarrow}-m$ is true. It is worth noting that, given $l.m$ and $-l.-m$, the assertion that $l{\rightarrow}m$ is false is equivalent to the assertion that $-l{\rightarrow}-m$ is true. Given $l.m$ and $-l.-m$, evidence that there is some relation between l and m, the assertion $l \rightarrow m$ is false does not mean there is no relation between l and m; it means that the relation has the form $-l \rightarrow -m$. The converse is of course true throughout. I am assuming that the baby has some built-in calculating mechanism that allows him to decide that $l.m$ and $-l.-m$ really occur. I am assuming that the baby has already ascertained the truth of the inequalities described above:

$$pl.m > p{-}l.m \quad \text{and} \quad p{-}l.{-}m > pl.{-}m$$

Note that I am insisting that instances of $-l$ and $-m$ are as important as instances of l and m. This is not true of most theories of learning.

That said, the information given by continuous reinforcement will not decide between the two hypotheses described above. The situation is ambiguous. Ambiguity is a fairly common occurrence in perception. Any new scene that is extended in three dimensions presents ambiguous binocular information. The organism is built to resolve such ambiguity, with automatic converging and diverging movements of the eyes, all an automatic consequence of the structure that detects binocular information. We might expect something analogous to occur in the operant learning situation. The experiment gives the baby only two of the three conjunctions predicted by either possible hypothesis. We might expect the baby to cast about furiously, looking for one of the other two conjunctions, either of which would clarify the situation. This does indeed occur (Figure 4-4).

We can simplify the baby's task by introducing NCR so that mobile movement will occur without a preceding leg movement; in this case $-l.m$ will occur. In this experiment CRF still occurs. However, the computer samples every hundredth of a second (centisecond, CS). If no

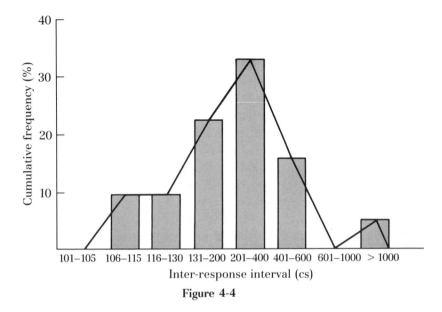

Figure 4-4

response is occurring and no reinforcement is occurring, the computer will deliver reinforcement with a given probability — in these experiments a probability of .2. This means the baby now has information that all of the pairings predicted by the hypothesis $l \rightarrow m$ do occur. Provided that the baby notices the events, there is no further information required for the baby to understand which is going on, given of course that the baby is using a construing system of the sort I have outlined.

On the reasoning presented here, and in previous publications (e.g., Bower, 1974) we might expect the baby to lose interest in the situation at this point. The situation is no longer ambiguous. The baby has satisfied his epistemic motives. If operant learning is like perception, we should expect the baby to become bored at this point. However, if our baby is a good, rational subject, he should try and disprove his hypothesis. (Good scientific practice, according to Popper, consists of formulating hypotheses and attempting to disprove them.) Our baby can show that he is operating on Popperian principles by testing to see whether $l.{-}m$ ever occurs. He would do this by increasing his rate of response to try to produce an instance of $l.{-}m$. This does occur. Figure 4-3 shows that this can happen, the proportion of "fast" responding increasing with the change from CRF to CRF + NCR.

In these experiments, reinforcement lasts 100 centiseconds. As

Figures 4-2 and 4-3 show, on these two schedules the baby antici-
pates the end of the reinforcement and, as predicted, on the CRF +
NCR schedule, changes the patterning of responses in a Popperian
way, as if trying to obtain an instance of $l.-m$. This pattern of
responding is quite contrary to predictions that would be made by
conventional behavior theory. NCR is not the most conventional
manipulation for a psychologist to attempt in the study of infant
learning. A more conventional manipulation is partial reinforcement,
in which not all responses lead to reinforcement. This must lead to
$l.-m$, the only conjunction that falsifies the hypothesis $l \rightarrow m$.

As we noted above, the assertion, in these conditions, that $l \rightarrow m$ is
false implies that $-l \rightarrow -m$ is true, that the hypothesis that states "if
my leg does not move, the mobile will not move" is true. This
hypothesis, like the other, predicts that three conjunctions will occur
and one will not. The predictions are

$$(l.m \vee -l.-m \vee l.-m).-(-l.m)$$

Thus, if we shift a baby from CRF to partial reinforcement, we provide
him with information that all of the predictions made by the hypothesis
$-l \rightarrow -m$ actually do occur. If our baby is a rational Popperian organism, again he should try to disprove the hypothesis by finding an
instance of $-l.m$. He can try to do this by withholding responses to see
whether the reinforcement ever occurs without a preceding behavior. As
figure 4-3 indicates, this kind of change in the patterning does occur, a
change once again that is quite contrary to conventional behavior theory.

These patterns are of interest in themselves. One could say that
the baby is searching for an event he has never experienced, repre-
senting something that has never been presented to him. Experiments of this kind could force us to rethink the whole idea of repre-
senting and representation in infancy. In the past, I have speculated
that a great deal of infant behavior that seems complex might be very
simple, no more than the result of the operation of a perceptual
system that is different from our own. That line of reasoning is clearly
invalidated by the behaviors just described. The infant is given information that one hypothesis is true, that one particular structure will
describe the presented events. Instead of being satisfied with what is,
the infant imagines the contrary, and tests for its validity. This is
clearly an instance of reflective abstraction, in the Piagetian sense
and, I am told, an instance of pure reflection in the Hegelian sense

(Kosok, 1976). The latter is particularly interesting since negation in that formal system uses the same reference base or content as affirmation, thus preserving, in our case, the relation between l and m that I have insisted on.

The notion that infants reflect on what is given is to me surprising. The idea that an infant can represent the contrary of what is astounds me, although not some others (e.g., Spitz, 1965). Unlikely as that seems, analysis of performance in the operant situation indicates that the baby does represent events that have not occurred, and that representation of the potential of possible events is a necessary component of any account of operant learning.

It might seem that the sketch I have given of what a baby is doing in an operant learning task is too complicated. In fact, as we shall see, the sketch is probably too simple. Nonetheless one might be able to account for the information given without invoking the apparatus of hypothesis testing used above. The surprising results above were the changes in response patterning consequent upon an instance of $l.-m$ or $-l.m$. One could work up an account of those surprising results by using the concept of "surprisal" (Attneave, 1959). Surprisal can be measured. It is inversely related to probability. The surprisal value of an event is conventionally taken as the logarithm to the base 2 of 1 divided by the probability, $\log_2 1/p$, or $-\log_2 p$. It is relatively easy to work out surprisal values in an operant situation. Take our baby, on CRF. Every leg kick produces a mobile movement, $l.m$, in our shorthand. Suppose after seven instances of $l.m$, the eighth limb movement produces no mobile movement, $l.-m$. The baby knows that once in eight times, l has not been followed by m. The probability of $l.-m$ is thus 1/8, so that the surprisal of $l.-m$ is $\log_2 1/(1/8) = 3$.

We can apply the same reasoning to instances of mobile movement not preceded by limb movement, $-l.m$. Suppose the baby has experienced seven instances of $l.m$, and then encounters one of $-l.m$. The surprisal of $-l.m$ works out again as $\log_2 1/(1/8) = 3$. Clearly an experimenter can pick any value of surprisal.

Now we must ask what is the normal effect of surprisal. Pavlov (1960) wrote at length about the behavioral consequences of surprise. They include stilling, suspension of breathing, orienting of the sense organs, and the like. In operant measures we would expect to see a drop in response rate. In the infant operant situation we do get this if we introduce a new, extraneous event, a one-second blast of noise. Response rate drops. Why then do we get an increase with −*l.m*? One could argue that the baby does not like surprise and is trying to protect himself from it. Surprise is associated with not making leg movements, −*l*, so the baby minimizes −*l* to minimize surprise, and hence increases the rate of response. One can take this explanation a fair way. However, I think it breaks down on examination of what happens on repetition of the surprising event. Suppose we go back to our baby who has experienced seven instances of *l.m* then one of −*l.m*. That first instance of −*l.m* has a surprisal of 3. Let that baby then experience another seven instances of *l.m* and then introduce another instance of −*l.m*. The surprisal of this second trial is

$$\log_2 1/(2/16) = 3$$

Surprisal value does not change. Over a series of trials one can keep surprisal constant, but the effect of the same amount of surprisal is not constant (Figure 4-5). The simplest way to account for the drop in the effect of surprisal is to accept that CRF is ambiguous. The occurrence of −*l.m* or *l.*−*m* will disambiguate the situation and allow the baby to adopt one of the two possible hypotheses. Subsequent instances of the disambiguating event will simply be further evidence for the hypothesis and should not be surprising at all.

The events occurring after CRF serve to disambiguate the situation, and to confirm one or other of the hypotheses that will account for the information given in CRF. The baby then, as we have seen, sets out to test the confirmed hypothesis by patterning his behavior to maximize the chances of finding a contradictory instance. What should happen if we provide the infant with a contradictory instance? Will the baby treat this as an extraneous event? A priori we might expect this to be the case. The infant has been given all of the information that is consonant with one hypothesis. Whichever hypothesis that is, it will be contradicted by the event we are discussing. The event in question is specifically excluded by the hypothesis under test; it should not happen, on the information given. Nonetheless the baby does carry on testing the hypothesis for prolonged periods. The Hegelian analysis (Kosok, op. cit.) would certainly suggest that the countercase is genuinely envisaged. So how would we know? I would suggest that if the baby responds to the new outcome uncertainty by producing the pattern of response that will minimize the

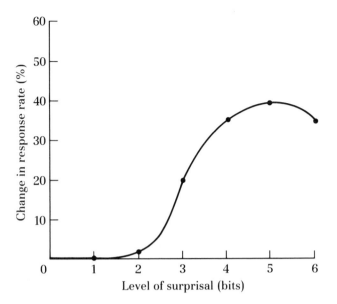

Figure 4-5

new source of uncertainty whether that results in an increase or a decrease in rate, then the baby is not treating the new event as extraneous. If it were seen as extraneous, then all that would happen would be surprise and a decrease in rate, as occurs with a genuinely extraneous event. Thus if the previously confirmed hypothesis is $l \rightarrow m$ and an instance of $l.-m$ is presented, the infant should increase the rate of $-l$, taking refuge with the familiar outcome uncertainty. Conversely if the confirmed hypothesis is $-l \rightarrow -m$ and an instance of $-l.m$ is presented, the baby should increase the rate of l, sticking with the familiar outcome uncertainty. This seems to be what does happen, at least under some circumstances. Table 4-2 presents the results from a group of eight-week-old infants who had had 200 seconds on a schedule confirming one or the other hypothesis. Interestingly here the baby seems to flip between hypotheses, depending on what has just happened. The flipping is quite prolonged, unlike the response to simple surprisal.

Schedules of this last kind are, it is claimed, more typical of the

71

Table 4-2 Percentage of change in response rate from a group of 8-week-old infants who had 200 seconds on a schedule confirming one or another hypothesis

Novel event	$-l.m$	$l.-m$
	+13	−18

Source: Fisher, 1986; Hopeton, 1986.

causal texture of the real world of the infant. In the real world, it is said, the infant's behaviors will elicit reinforcement on a partial schedule, with noncontingent delivery of the same reinforcement. Watson (1985) has been particularly keen on this kind of schedule.

Watson and Bower, in discussion around 1976, came up with the hypothesis that the infant in daily life would come to expect mixed schedules, so that this kind of alteration between hypotheses would cease. The most "attractive" schedules would be those that deviated slightly from the expected schedule, just as a slight modification of a familiar visual shape is more attractive than the standard shape. On this reasoning the infant would be disturbed on a schedule on which he was less *or more* successful than past experience had led him to expect he would be. Early experience could thus have profound effects on later learning. Perfect contingency, on this reasoning, would be very disturbing and would not lead to learning. This hypothesis is akin to the "perceptual" hypothesis of learning that we saw reason to question above. While it is clearly relevant to long-term stability, the main focus of this book, there are other hypotheses designed to predict the outcomes of such mixed schedules.

A line of thought that I find attractive is derived from Piaget. Thus far I have been assuming that the infant tries to fit events into a logical framework that is similar to that of the adult. The adult logical system is characterized by three rules, the "laws of thought":

1. *Identity:* A proposition implies itself ($p \rightarrow p$).

2. *Excluded middle:* A proposition is either true or false.

3. *Noncontradiction:* A proposition cannot be both true and false.

Piaget (1938) suggested that the logical system of the infant might lack one of the latter two laws. Toward the end of his life (Piaget, 1981) he suggested that the infant operated without either the law of excluded middle or the law of noncontradiction. The baby would thus operate with a four-valued logic, the values of which make a semi-lattice, as shown in Figure 4-6. Value is almost as before, with *true* highest and *false* lowest. The two new values are equal but incommensurable, that is, they cannot be compared with one another, so an equation with one on one side of the symbol and the other on the other is logically meaningless.

Clearly if Piaget was correct in asserting that the infant operates with a four-valued logic, the infant has other ways of dealing with contingent pairings. I would propose that long-term continuous reinforcement in my experiment would result in $l \rightarrow m$ being given the value "neither true nor false" simply because neither $-l.m$ nor $l.-m$ ever occur. A mixed schedule on the other hand gives evidence that $l \rightarrow m$ is true and that it is false, $l \rightarrow m.-(l \rightarrow m)$. On Piaget's hypothesis, $l \rightarrow m$ should thus attain the value, "both true and false." What effect would this have? On the reasoning presented thus far, we might expect a drop to a very low rate of response; an hypothesis that is "both true and false" can never be proved or disproved; any event fits with it; it predicts all possible events; it is epistemically saturated; since it is widely agreed that infants are epistemically motivated, motivation to perform should thus disappear.

There is a much more interesting consequence of Piaget's hypothesis. A proposition that is "both true and false" cannot be asserted or denied. It thus can never be put into an implicative relation with any other proposition. Any relation that is "both true and false" will

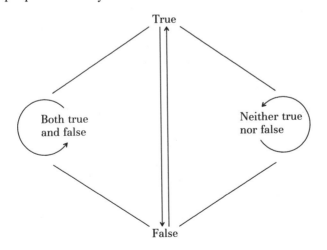

Figure 4-6

remain isolated from the rest of experience, impervious to proof or disproof, irrelevant to everything else in life. While I think this is intuitively obvious, it can be proved (Mackinson, 1973). Accepting that a relation $l \rightarrow m$ is both true and false does not mean that there is no relation between l and m. It means that there is a relation of a particular form, a form that isolates the relation from the rest of the psychological world, and renders it irrelevant to everything else. The baby could thus learn a skill, some behavior outcome relation; if the relation had the value both true and false, it would stay in the growing child's repertoire, but isolated forever from his other concerns.

Clearly this kind of process could be relevant to long-term effects in development. The first association that sprang to my mind was Bowlby's description of some affectionless psychopaths, individuals who have a full range of social skills, charm, even, with those social skills existing in isolation, cut off from the rest of their world, independent of their system of understanding the world. Bowlby, of course, proposed that affectionless psychopathy stems from experiences in infancy. It is surely possible that the baby has learned some social skills, that these skills are irrelevant, and thus that the relations involved have the valuation "both true and false."

There is a more everyday instance of a true and false behavior outcome relationship: crying for attention. As all parents know, all babies cry from time to time. Sometimes the baby wants to be fed, sometimes the baby wants to be changed, sometimes the baby wants social attention. Most parents, in my experience, try to meet all of these demands, initially. However, soon parental exhaustion supervenes and the baby is rationed. In other words, crying is put on a reinforcement schedule. Not all instances of crying are reinforced. The baby's crying is on a partial reinforcement schedule. Behavior theorists do not recommend this since on that view the outcome should be an increase in the rate of crying. What is the baby to make of this? The baby could reasonably formulate an initial hypothesis "whenever I cry, I get attention", an hypothesis we can symbolize as $c \rightarrow a$. This hypothesis will be falsified as soon as the parents begin the partial reinforcement schedule. On a perfect partial schedule the baby could only conclude the alternate hypothesis "unless I cry, I do not get attention", symbolized as $-c \rightarrow -a$, a representation that means that $c \rightarrow a$ is false. However, parents are not perfect reinforcement schedules. I am sure that all parents deliver noncontingent reinforcement as well, driven by worry about what the silence means. This occurs all through early parenting. The rate of crying will be increased by this kind of manipulation, noncontingent reinforcement, on the reasoning presented here, even though that reasoning runs counter to the warnings of behavior theory. However, we can assume that most parents will put their baby on a partial reinforcement schedule, ignoring some of the episodes of crying, but they will also introduce some noncontingent reinforcement, checking the baby, attending to the baby, even when there has been no crying. The outcome can only be a decision that $c \rightarrow a$ is both true and false. The time taken to get to that point will depend on the relative frequency of the various conjunctions. It should come as a relief to parents when that point is reached since the absolute frequency of crying should go down, since there is no more information to be obtained about the $c \rightarrow a$ relation: more important, there should be no attempt to embed crying in more complex relations.

This outcome, while desirable, is very much an imagined object of desire. There are few systematic data on crying, the classic paradigm, which like most classics is often cited but not studied. There are, however, data on other skills, two of which I would like to consider. These are auditory guided reaching and imitation. The former has mostly been studied in an applied context, with blind infants, although there have been some studies done with sighted infants in darkness. The two will be treated as equivalent in what follows.

A young baby, in the neonate range, when presented with a noise-making object, will attempt to grasp the object. The frequency of this behavior declines to almost zero by 20 weeks of age. After that age the behavior becomes very hard to elicit and will probably never be seen again, certainly not in the functional contexts where one sees visually guided reaching. Let us look at auditory guided reaching in a logical framework. The behavior can be described as "whenever a sound specifying a source in space occurs, the source can be manually explored." We can write this as

$$s \rightarrow m$$

The nature of the human organism, and the vicissitudes of everyday life will conspire to ensure that this relation will soon acquire the value "both true and false." The human perceptual system cannot register the origin of sounds with sufficient accuracy to ensure manual contact. It will thus happen that sounds occur that cannot be contacted, giving the conjunction $s.-m$. Likewise there are many manually explorable objects in the world that do not emit sounds, and the baby is bound to contact them sooner or later, producing the conjunction $-s.m$. The baby will thus be exposed to the conjunctions $s.m$, $s.-m$, $-s.m$, $-s.-m$. The relation $s \rightarrow m$ is thus both true and false. Therefore it cannot be fitted into a relation with anything else. The baby thus would not reach for a sound-defined object in order to put it in his mouth, or in relation with another object, or anything else. Any such activity would be the projection of a relation of the form $(s \rightarrow m) \rightarrow x$ and such relations cannot be projected.

I am convinced that something of this kind does go on. Certainly $s \rightarrow m$ relations are deleted from the blind baby's repertoire quite rapidly. Despite devoted clinical attention they do not, it seems to me, recur. The usual reaching on sound cue seen in blind children is not reaching at all, but rather a stereotyped clasping at the midline plane, the imaginary surface that vertically bisects the human body. Essential functions, where the hand would normally be used, may be carried out without it. Mouthing and even eating may occur without the use of the hand as an intermediary.

Sound may be a prototype for all exterospecific stimulation. As we saw in Chapter 2, the young baby certainly can treat all stimuli from the outside world as equivalent in some fashion. The functional failure of sight restoration operations may thus be less of a puzzle than it might seem. The reasoning outlined above would apply in the same way if "sounds" above were replaced by an "exterospecific stimulus." Since visual inputs are exterospecific, they could be classed as irrelevant before they had ever been experienced. Indeed, depending on the precise way in which the elements are categorized by the baby, simple auditory-manual experience could result in cognitive lesions extending even to such far-off skills as those involved in Euclidean geometry.

Furthermore, the lesions would persist if they stemmed from a "true and false" assignment. Remember, it is impossible to negate that logical value (Figure 4-6). No biasing of experience can change it; the assignment "true" can be contradicted; the assignment "false" can be contradicted; but the assignment "true and false" cannot be contradicted, or corrected.

I am not arguing here that auditorily guided reaching must be deleted from the repertoire. My own observations of many blind babies have convinced me that the behavior is subject to the kind of mixed schedule that would ultimately lead to the evaluation of the stimulus-response relation as both true and false. Blind infants and children could thus persist in reaching, but not put the reaching into any larger framework of behavior or understanding.

While I do not want to get into the morass of the relation between action and thought, it does not seem implausible that the lesions in spatial thinking exhibited by the congenitally blind child have their origins in the logical evaluation of their earliest spatial behaviors.

The effect of early blindness was one of the paradigm cases mentioned earlier in this chapter. The other paradigm case involved social behaviors touched on above.

Thus far I have said nothing about how long-term benign effects attain their stability. It is clear that it can hardly be by some process parallel to that proposed for malign effects. The essence of that process is that some psychological process comes to be seen as irrelevant to the rest of mental life. The essence of the benign effect is that it is relevant in the beginning, then becomes functionally irrelevant — irrelevant to the outside world of the organism at that time — but still can be reawakened whenever the outside world changes. To explain this I would appeal to one psychological principle and one other idea from logic. The psychological principle is that young infants treat, categorize, perceive events in the broadest possible way, with development being very much a differentiation or specification of these initial categories. Thus infants respond to exterospecific stimuli, not even noticing whether or not they are carried by light, sound, smell, or whatever. They respond to people as a class, not to persons. With development this broad response becomes specific; there is a visual world, an auditory world, there are big people, little people, familiar people, strangers, and so on. That such a process of differentiation and specification goes on is, I believe, as well established a principle of development as one can find (Bower, 1982; 1984).

The logical notion I wish to introduce, from modal logic, is that of possible worlds. This was introduced to make sense of certain logical puzzles we need not address. For our purposes we need only look at one axiom, which is as follows: a statement (people are responsive whenever one is affectionate) is true in some possible worlds if and only if the negation of that statement is not true in all possible worlds.

Let us now return to our sighted child who has stably operated with what, in shorthand, I call an idea of stable three-dimensional space, subsuming successful reaching, locating, etc. Suppose the child is blinded, losing at a stroke all of these abilities. The child by this stage probably by one year has differentiated perceptual worlds. He knows that the world he is now in is different from the world he was in. He knows that there are two possible worlds, and that three-dimensional order thus remains true. The clearest examples of this that I have seen are not sighted children who have been blinded but blind-born children who are given a sonic guide to use as a surrogate for vision. This device permits very normal development in blind babies (e.g., Aitken and Bower, 1982b).

What is noteworthy is that babies who have used the machine to discover the layout of the world, or a part of it, will spontaneously remove the machine and try to fit the information they can get into the known framework. One of these children, seen by thousands on television (Bower, 1984) makes extremely inventive use of echoes she can produce with her voice and feet. In all situations, with or without her machine, she shows in her behavior and her burgeoning language, an awareness of the stability and order of the world, characteristics she can only perceive intermittently with her machine. This child lives in two worlds but never forgets the structure of the better one. Sight restoration has been successful fifty years after the initial loss of vision, a tribute to the persistence of such possible worlds (Gregory, 1963).

Let's take a child who has stably acquired the belief that people are affectionate and responsive. Suppose he is now with people who are not. He knows the difference. He knows that there are two possible worlds. Whenever he meets new people he will want to find out which world they are from. To deal with them, he has the resources acquired in both worlds. With luck he will eventually find people who come from the good world, remaining forever aware of the darker side of human nature.

I would like to summarize what I am proposing. The human infant is built to detect certain event characteristics of the world. I have argued for the nature of these characteristics elsewhere. The infant is also built to detect conjunctions between events. Observed conjunctions will be fitted into a predictive framework that can be described as a logical structure. In this chapter I have focused on the "→" structure. Other structures might be more satisfactory. The fit of that structure to the world will be tested actively as far as it is within the baby's powers. From real-world testing, a framework will be assigned one of three values. The value assigned will determine whether that frame can stand in a predictive relationship to events or other frames, or whether any such relation is itself vacuous, empty, of no predictive power, neither possibly true nor possibly false. The rogue value, of course, is both true and false, an evaluation which must obviously be permanent since there is no way in which it can be contradicted. With development, the child will become aware directly that there are different values for the same frame in different worlds.

I should emphasize that I am not proposing that there is a change in the logical construing system of the developing child. I am proposing that with development it becomes easier and easier to differentiate contexts in which one hypothesis will be appropriate from contexts in which the inverse will apply. This kind of learning is possible in the neonate period, as Lipsitt has shown, and will, I propose, become easier with development. My own impression of babies faced with a mixed schedule generated by a computer is that they are trying to work out under what circumstances one hypothesis applies versus another. They cannot succeed but persist in trying for long periods. This openness may eventually be lost, to yield the rigid adult who does not even notice information that contradicts his hypotheses.

Certainly many older infants register dislike of such schedules by walking or crawling out of the situation. This cannot be because the schedules are strange; Watson (1985) is undoubtedly correct in asserting that mixed schedules are characteristic of the world the infant lives in. However, in a laboratory there is no way to work out when one hypothesis is true and when it is false; it is obvious that this is impossible, so stripped down are the surroundings. The introduction of possible modal cues might maintain the babies' interest. In the real world there is always a plethora of potential information, so there is always a possibility of ultimate disambiguation.

What is the "status" of the kind of explanation I am offering here? This question rarely, if ever, comes up with discussing "mental" change, as in discussing the origins of affectionlessness. However, in discussions of early blindness, sooner or later people begin talking about the anatomy of the brain, as if neural changes somehow provided a truer explanation of the psychological changes under discussion. I have strong practical objections to this line of argument as well as an objection of principle.

The practical objections, in the context to visual handicap, stem from the failure of neurophysiological information to aid either understanding or therapy of individual blind children or adults. Specifically there are many cases documented in the literature of sight restoration operations which have been neurophysiological successes but psychological, functional failures (Valvo, 1971). Conversely there are cases where, on neurophysiological criteria, there is no vision yet where there is perfectly adequate functional vision. Of the latter, the case I know best is that of a pair of twin boys. Neither showed any cortical visual evoked potential at all. Of their four eyes, one showed an electroretinogram (ERG) of 1 percent of normal amplitude, the others nothing at all. And yet they could see at a functional level (Nielson, 1982). In their case the neurophysiological evidence nearly led to disastrous medical and educational consequences. My point is that neurophysiological indicators are very misleading guides to action with the whole organism. This point has been forcefully put by such eminent neurophysiologists as Wiesel (1967) and Gaze (1971). The latter has said that he would never try to infer properties of a part (the brain) from properties of the whole organism, nor properties of the whole from properties of the part. In his own work he has found too much noncorrespondence (Gaze, 1971).

The principled objection is that facts in one domain cannot explain facts in another domain, any more than a basket of oranges explains a basket of apples. What I am trying to do here is to use logic to explain how particular psychological inputs come to have particular psychological outputs. No answer will be found by looking for neurological correlates of these inputs. A change in descriptive terminology is never an explanation.

What has gone before might seem unduly pessimistic in regard to the possibility of correcting or reversing an acquisition that has gone wrong, an acquisition that has been evaluated as both true and false, and therefore independent of the rest of mental life. This pessimism is unjustified as I shall show in later chapters. The view to be developed is extremely optimistic, certainly far more so than the quasi-neurological speculations outlined in the last paragraphs.

······

5

The Logical Infant

In this chapter I would like to take another look at what I think is the most surprising claim made in the last chapter, the claim that infants are logical.

It seems highly probable that human beings are logical for at least part of their lives; the problem is to define the part. There is controversy over the claim that the ability to reason logically leaves us in our mid-thirties (Welford, 1958). There is even more controversy over when in development the logical lightening strikes. Investigations, largely inspired by Piaget (1942a), have indicated that logical reasoning is attained in mid-adolescence, and probably not before then (Inhelder and Piaget, 1958). The idea that logical reasoning is a difficult and late attainment is congenial to many psychologists, most of whom, after all, are past their mid-thirties. There is, however, no consensus that logical reasoning is such a late bloom. Chomsky (1985), Fodor (1975), and to a lesser extent Bower (1979) have all argued, on logical grounds, that a powerful logic must be in place from the beginning of psychological life, and indeed that the developmental process might be a downhill path, not just from mid-adolescence but from birth itself. Piaget himself argued from the 1930s that at least some of the laws of thought must be built into the structure of the developing nervous system (Piaget, 1936). More recently, with Monnier (1981), he presented data indicating that babies around one year of age could use a logical calculus formally similar to that attributed to late adolescents. In one of his very last papers he argued for a very economic and powerful logic, relevance logic (Anderson and Belknapp, 1976) as the basic program for cognitive development (Piaget, 1982).

When we speak of a human being as logical, we are asserting that that human uses argument forms that are embedded in one or another logical system to make deductions that will serve as guides to action. There are different logical systems that provide us with different paradigms against which to evaluate the deductive processes we can infer from the behavior of a human. In this chapter I will consider three possible systems. The first of these is the classical two-valued logic we are all familiar with. In this system a proposition can have two values only, *true* or *false*, and every proposition must have one of these values. This whole complex system is based on three axioms, the so-called laws of thought. These are the law of identity (if a statement is true, it is true, i.e., $p = p$), the law of noncontradiction [a statement cannot be both true and false, i.e., $-(p.-p)$], and the law of excluded middle [a statement is either true or false, i.e., $(p \lor -p)$].

Piaget in 1936 argued that development could proceed without the last of these. In essence Piaget was proposing a three-valued logic for development. This dispenses with one of the assumptions of classical logic, at the cost of increasing the number of values involved to three. The three values are *true, false*, and *neither true nor false*. At the end of his life, Piaget (1982) threw out the law of noncontradiction as well, endorsing a one-axiom system with four values, *true, false, neither true nor false*, and *both true and false* (see Figure 4-6).

For the purpose of this book, elementary psychological events can only be true or false, which is to say they either happen or they do not. However, any organism, even a baby, can formulate a hypothesis about the relation between events. That hypothesis, one step removed from experience, can take on any of the four values shown in Figure 4-6.

I propose that if we have two events — let us call them p and q — that show a particular pattern of co-occurrence, the organism will hypothesize that there is some relation between p and q. The organism will try to specify the nature of the relation between p and q. Given that p and q ($p.q$) co-occur and that the absence of p goes with the absence of q ($-p.-q$), the organism can decide that one of two possible hypotheses is true. These hypotheses, remember, are $p \rightarrow q$ or $-p \rightarrow -q$. If $-p.q$ occurs, then $p \rightarrow q$ is true and $-p \rightarrow -q$ is false; if the third conjunction encountered is $p.-q$, then $p \rightarrow q$ is false and $-p \rightarrow -q$ is true. The organism knows that there is a relation between p and q. Asserting that $p \rightarrow q$ is false does not invalidate the relation; it boils down to saying that $-p \rightarrow -q$ is true. As we saw in the last chapter, we can set things up in the laboratory to force our subject to accept one of the intermediate values. The same thing can happen in more realistic situations.

Consider the simple task shown in Figure 5-2. Success in this task marks the child's attainment of Piaget's stage VI of the object concept. It is a relatively late attainment, coming into the child's repertoire around twenty months of age. Children younger than this will consistently fail on this task, even when tested longitudinally (Wishart and Bower, 1985). Such infants can however pass a rather simpler task shown in Figure 5-1. This task is the test for transition from Piaget's stage IV to his stage V of object concept development. The transition usually occurs around ten months of age. I would propose that a baby who passes the IV–V transition task and fails the V–VI transition task is using a rule of the following sort. "Whenever an object loses its own boundaries in relation with another object — vanishes — it will be found where it was last seen with intact boundaries" [for a justification of this terminology, see Wishart and Bower 1984]. This hypothesis involves an *antecedent* event and a *consequent* prediction, with a resultant behavior; retrieval of the "vanished" object. The "whenever" relation between the two propositions above, the antecedent and the consequent, is symbolized by "$\rightarrow$". If we let p stand for the antecedent in the italicized hypothesis above, and q for the consequent, the hypothesis can be written in the standard logical form $p \rightarrow q$. As a deductive form, and therefore as a guide to action, the hypothesis has the characteristics shown in the

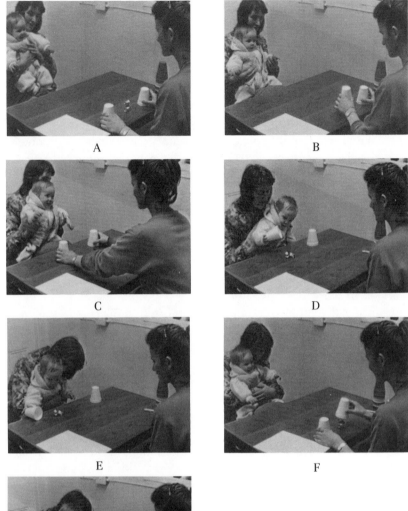

Figure 5-1 In this task the baby sees a toy hidden under one cup. He is allowed to retrieve it. After one more repetition the toy is then hidden under the other cup.

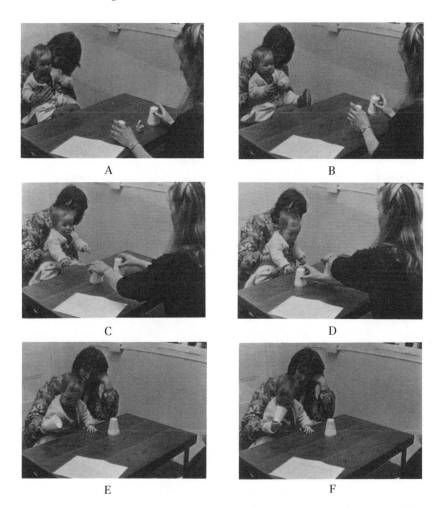

Figure 5-2 In this task the baby sees a toy hidden under one of two cups. The cups are then transposed and the baby allowed to search for the toy.

following truth table:

	an object vanishes	the object will be seen where it was last seen,		$-(p \rightarrow q) =$
	p	q	$p \rightarrow q$	$\neg p \rightarrow \neg q$
1.	true	true	true	true
2.	false	true	true	false
3.	true	false	false	true
4.	false	false	true	true

This shows the truth values for the denial of the hypothesis, the assertion that $p \rightarrow q$ is *false*. Note what was said above about the relation between these two hypotheses.

Let us assume that the baby confronted with the task in Figure 5-1 believes that $p \rightarrow q$ is *true*. We have the following description of the task:

belief	$p \rightarrow q$	is *true*
event	p	has occurred and is *true*
∴prediction	q	will be *true*
∴behavior	r	is successful (*true*)

Translation of the prediction into behavioral success, retrieval, gives us another argument: $(p \rightarrow q) \rightarrow r$. This can be translated into ordinary language as "if the hypothesis is true, the object will be retrieved." ("If . . . , then . . ." and "whenever . . . , then . . ." are both ordinary language equivalents of the symbol $\rightarrow$). The truth table of $(p \rightarrow q) \rightarrow r$ is as follows:

	$(p \rightarrow q)$	r	$(p \rightarrow q) \rightarrow r$
1.	true	true	true
2.	false	true	true
3.	true	false	false
4.	false	false	true

What happens, though, when the same hypothesis is applied to the task shown in Figure 5-2? In this case the object will not be retrieved. This implies, by the classic argument, *modus tollens*, that the hypothesis is false.

$$(p \rightarrow q) \rightarrow r$$
$$-r$$
$$\therefore -(p \rightarrow q)$$

The baby can adjust his hypotheses to take account of this, ending up with $(-p \rightarrow -q) \rightarrow r$.

What will happen then if the child operates on the belief that $p \rightarrow q$ is *false*, that $-p \rightarrow -q$ is *true*. We have the sequence

belief	$p \rightarrow q$	is *false*, i.e., $-p \rightarrow -q$ is *true*
event	p	has occurred and is *true*
∴prediction	$q \lor -q$	

In other words, the object is either where it was last seen or it is somewhere else. This may not seem a terribly useful prediction but it is the only one the babies can make, if they are logical, and they are logical, judging by their behavior. It is very common for a baby presented with this task to get a 100 percent string of errors over several sessions, which is what would result from a belief that the hypothesis was true. This will be replaced by looking where the object was — as before — looking in all sorts of other places, in the experimenter's hand, under the table, on his or her mother's lap, and occasionally in the location where the object actually is. When the baby is behaving this way, one can even demonstrate the logic of the baby by eliciting the most illogical-seeming behavior. Suppose that one signals the baby that the trial is about to begin. Suppose one then simply places the object between the two cups, so that it is still visible, in no spatial relation with any other object. One can then see the infant search under both cups, search the experimenter's hand, look on the floor, all this, seemingly, for an object that sits in solitary state, fully available for retrieval (Figure 5-3). How does this "illogical" behavior demonstrate that the baby is logical? Consider the sequence

belief	$p \rightarrow q$	is *false*, i.e., $-p \rightarrow -q$
event	$-p$	the object is not in spatial relation with another
∴prediction	$-q$	the object is *not* where it was (and still can be) seen alone

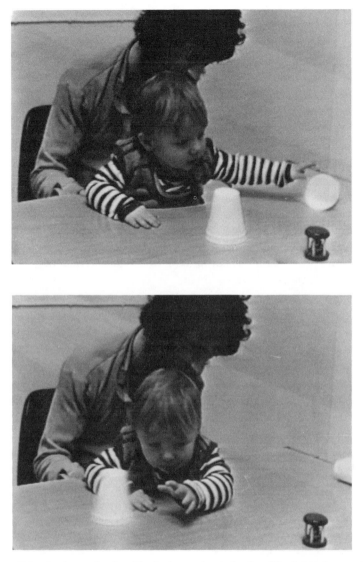

Figure 5-3 Logic can lead to illogical-seeming behavior. The infant is searching for a toy which is in full view.

This last prediction can only lead to the odd behavior described above, whose lack of success — retrieval — must surely tend to weaken the belief that $p \rightarrow q$ is *false*.

One might wonder why, when the baby occasionally does retrieve the object at the other cup-defined location, he or she does not simply get better and better rather than sticking at a low level of success guaranteed by operating on the hypothesis that $p \rightarrow q$ is *false*. If babies were S-R reinforcement machines I am sure they would show this gradual pattern of improvement. However, they do not, which, for me is evidence that the baby is a logical organism, deducing predictions from hypotheses, with the existence of a testable hypothesis necessary for any systematic behavior at all.

How then does the baby advance? He or she knows that the hypothesis is not *true*. He or she knows that it is not *false*. He or she can only conclude that his or her hypothesis is *neither true nor false*. In other words he or she must make use of a third logical value. The original hypothesis is *neither true nor false*. In other words it is irrelevant. To comprehend this problem situation, the baby must formulate a new hypothesis for testing. I do not intend to pursue what happens for this is not a chapter on "the object concept." However, I would emphasize that the baby, where we have left him or her, has just made a significant advance. He or she has discovered that a cherished hypothesis is irrelevant. This is a necessary discovery for subsequent advance. It is also a difficult step to make. The most mature scientists often or usually find it difficult to admit that their hypotheses are irrelevant.

If the baby is using this extra logical value, we have a ready-made explanation of some other oddities in behavior. There are some arguments that are true in a two-valued logic that are not true in higher-valued systems of logic. For example, the argument: $a \vee b. -a, \therefore b$. This is the disjunctive syllogism. It is not valid in any save two-valued logic. Likewise, transitive inference (i.e., $p \rightarrow q$, $q \rightarrow r$, $\therefore p \rightarrow r$) only works in a two-valued logic. The lack of validity of the disjunctive syllogism maybe explains why babies in two-choice tasks like those described above, having made an error, do not immediately correct themselves; why indeed they fail the classic Piagetian inference task (see Wishart and Bower, 1984). As for transitive inference, Mounoud and Bower (1974) did not find it in one-year-olds and it is not exactly easy to demonstrate even in three-year-olds (Bryant and Trabasso, 1971).

In the last chapter we looked at an operant conditioning situation. A situation such that when a baby's leg moves, a mobile moves. The baby might, in time, reasonably formulate the hypothesis, "whenever my leg moves up, the mobile moves." This formulation would be reasonable in the light of the information given and some prior hypotheses the baby would bring to the experiment (Bower, 1979). If the baby did formulate such an hypothesis, its overall form would be

	l	m	$l \to m$
1.	true	true	true
2.	false	true	true
3.	true	false	false
4.	false	false	true

It is noteworthy that babies in such a situation do attempt to work through the four tests of the hypothesis shown in the above table. In so doing, they display behavior that many observers would dismiss as pointless, indeed illogical. Some babies, having discovered that an upward leg movement results in mobile movement, will engage in frequent vigorous downward leg movements, straining to produce a nonupward leg movement. This behavior is pointless in the context of reinforcement theory. It is not at all pointless if the baby is systematically testing an hypothesis. By producing $-l$ the baby can check the truth-value of lines 2 and 4 of the truth table above, and thereby test the validity of the hypothesis in a way that concentration on line 2 would render impossible. This kind of systematic testing is most obvious in babies around twelve months of age, but it can be seen in subjects as young as eight weeks (Monnier, op. cit.)

The operant situation will allow us to specify the quantitative parameters of the supposed process. The baby must require some information to decide that there is a relation between p and q, or l and m in my standard situation. At present that amount is unknown. Pilot work indicates that babies exposed to a CRF schedule linking l and m all show the appropriate changes in rate consequent on $l.-m$ or $-l.m$ after seven pairings of $l.m$. With lesser numbers there is no such certainty. The surprisal value of $l.-m$ or $-l.m$ after seven instances of $l.m$ is 3. With a surprisal value of 2, we have found no consistent pattern of change consequent on the novel event (Petrie, Symonds and Bower, in prep). The operant situation will also allow us to work out whether or not CRF is a necessary first step in learning, and what proportions of contradictory examples are tolerated before the baby assumes that there is no relation between l and m. Clearly no relation exists if the four possible pairings $l.m$, $l.-m$, $-l.-m$, and $-l.m$ are all equally probable. How far toward equality can the probabilities go? It would be interesting to know.

I have no doubt that a great deal of psychological work remains to be done to define, for example, the frequencies attaching to each conjunction that are necessary to the $p.-p$ outcome. I am sure that under some circumstances evidence in favor of one or the other value would be so slight that it would be suppressed, as happens in adulthood (Festinger, 1957). If babies do not suppress contradiction, what do they do? Young babies accept it and will continue to work away in the situation, trying, one supposes, to find an hypothesis that is true and covers the information given. In the situation outlined here they could do so, with difficulty. The time spent on the effort provides an insight into what Piaget meant when he talked of contradiction as the motor of development (Piaget, 1979). Older babies, we should note, do not settle down with the same equanimity. When *both true and false* become the only value possible, these babies tend to try to leave the experimental situation (Monnier, op. cit.). This may reflect a growing commitment to the convenience of two-valued logic, a possibility we will take up below.

The operant situation also will allow us to work out what is going on in the mind of the baby before the baby shows us that he has grasped the hypothesis we are trying to teach him. As noted just above, we have data indicating that, after seven presentations o. ˈg movement and mobile movement, the baby has worked out tʰ ˈ there is a relation between leg movement and mobile movemen Before that, what does the baby think is going on? I would propose, as I have before (Bower, 1979), that the baby's first hypothesis would be that there is a relation between his movement and the event in the outside world. We could write that hypothesis as follows:

$$\text{my movement is related to mobile movement}$$
$$m \; R \; m \tag{1}$$

That general or abstract hypothesis could rapidly be specified to

$$\text{my limb movement is related to mobile movement}$$
$$l \; R \; m \tag{2}$$

eventually coming to the familiar

$$\text{leg movement is related to mobile movement}$$
$$l \; R \; m \tag{3}$$

Chapter 4 was mostly devoted to the baby at line (3). As we saw there, the baby tries to specify the relation between l and m, to discover whether it is $l \rightarrow m$ or $-l \rightarrow -m$. That attempt at specification goes on, but there are also attempts to specify the nature of the operant, to discover which leg, whether upward movements are required, and so on (see especially Monnier, 1981). This specification is analogous to that described in Chapter 2 as characteristic of perceptual processes. I should like to emphasize one point. The three relations given above exist at logically different levels, in such a way that equation (1) could be true while equations (2) or (3) bore no relation to the actual state of affairs. We might thus extinguish equation (3) without affecting equations (1) or (2). In terms of countering early acquisitions, this logical property of the various stages or phases of learning would surely pose problems. Thus a child who had learned to fear all men might learn that a particular man was not dangerous; this last item of learning would leave the previous hypothesis intact.

In the same way the infant could learn that a class of behaviors produces consequences that he desires. Thus the baby could learn that hostile behavior makes people go away. The extinction of a particular hostile behavior would not extinguish the more abstract hypothesis that is organized around hostile behavior in general. Perhaps in this way we can understand the results of Page (1955) described in Chapter 3; he found, remember, that forced extinction of a particular response to a fear-inducing stimulus did not affect the rest of the gamut of fear-induced behaviors elicited by that stimulus.

In general I am arguing that because extinction, by definition, follows acquisition, it will have a *narrower* focus than acquisition. What is acquired may be at a logically different level from what is extinguished. The original acquisition may thus persist and last in the teeth of successive extinctions of more particular hypotheses derived from it. This necessary characteristic of learning and extinction would clearly apply with more force to the acquisitions of infancy, since those acquisitions are necessarily general, as I argued in Chapter 2. However, we need not assume that this kind of effect, this source of long-term stability, can only operate in infancy. It is possible that all learning has this characteristic (see e.g., Bateson, 1972).

It would seem that four-valued logic as a mode of construing the world may not outlast infancy, or not by very much. The young child begins to solve problems that are insoluble in a four-valued logic, to reject problems that require a four-valued logic. There seems to be a distinct change of the mind toward the end of infancy. On the logical models we have considered, the change would seem to involve the adoption or incorporation of the two additional laws of thought — the law of excluded middle and the law of noncontradiction — as rules for construing hypotheses about the world. This is no minor step. The amount of the infant's random access memory taken up by content-less assumptions is tripled. The cost is thus considerable. The gain is the reduction in the number of truth values that can be assigned to hypotheses about the world, a reduction from four to two.

This does not seem a massive gain, although, by making some inferences possible, it may simplify the world to a great extent. This latter gain, as we have seen, does have costs. The infant becomes less open to certain kinds of experience, less able to discard hypotheses and start afresh, less able to tolerate contradictions in experience. Where then is the gain? The gain, I feel, is in the control of action. Action is by its nature two-valued. One either acts or one does not. There are no intermediates of action. Perhaps then as the infant becomes more capable of acting in the world, the demands of action force the adoption of a two-valued logic. Four-valued logic may thus be a luxury, available to the contemplative infant and a few contemplative philosophers. For the rest of us it may vanish in the labor and heat of everyday life.

The clearest evidence that there is some change is found in Monnier's work (op. cit.). The oldest infants in her studies would not accept conjunctions of events in a conditioning situation that would require them to suspend one or another of the three laws of thought; thus a mixed schedule would produce a walkout. I doubt that this kind of behavior really marks a change in the mental structure of the infant. There are adult philosophers and psychologists, such as Piaget himself, who can operate with three- and four-valued systems of logic. However, in the normal world they are not useful. Two-valued logics are useful and it is their utility in the real world that may account for their grip on the imagination of Western humanity.

In essence I am proposing a strong analogy between infants and adults in some respects. Infants, like adults, can detect contingent relations between events. I am proposing that these contingent relations are represented in the baby's mind as "if . . . then . . ." hypotheses. The hypothesis in the baby's mind will be more general, more abstract than the hypothesis in the adult mind, given the same

information; this a consequence of the undifferentiated infant perceptual system (Chapter 2). The baby will then seek for information to
specify the initial hypothesis, to change its value from *neither true
nor false* to *true* or to *false*. Having worked out an hypothesis that fits
the information given, the baby will seek information that would
contradict the hypothesis under test. Given that such information is
not forthcoming, the baby, I propose, will accept the hypothesis, with
its contents, as a valid guide for action.

Action may force a change in the hypothesis. Data may emerge
that indicates a given hypothesis is *both true and false* or *neither true
nor false*. This is equivalent to saying that there is a relation between
the two hypotheses but its form is indeterminable; it cannot act as a
guide to action. If action is required, a new hypothesis will be formed,
under the goad of action. The original hypothesis will persist, im-
mune to proof or disproof, isolated from everything else.

That the baby should entertain such evaluations of hypotheses in
no way marks the baby as different from or inferior to the adult. The
physicist E. Schroedinger explained modern physics in terms of a cat
in a box. One must be able to imagine that the cat is alive, or dead, or
both alive and dead, or neither dead nor alive. These infantile notions are thus still in play at the very frontiers of human knowledge.

6

The Object Concept

In this chapter I would like to bring together some of the ideas developed in previous chapters. The ideas in question are first, that the perceptual system of the young infant is more abstract, less specific, less differentiated than that of the older infant or adult; the learning of the young infant is thus more general than the adult would expect, on his or her perception of the information given. Second, I would like to assume that the mind of the young infant operates on rational principles, principles that may be different from those we use, but rational nonetheless. These principles, I have already argued, operate in all areas of development, and can operate on the abstract information given by the young perceptual system. One well-studied topic in development shows up both of these characteristics of the early human perceptual cognitive system; that topic is the development of the object concept.

Since Piaget first pointed out that infants have problems with some tasks involving objects, the development of the set of skills that are taken to mark attainment of the object concept has fascinated psychologists. For a long time most English-speaking psychologists worked on the problem as if it were a problem of representation, the baby's difficulty being summarized as "out of sight is out of mind." Chapter 1 of Piaget's *The Child's Construction of Reality* does focus on hiding tasks. However in Chapter 2, Piaget points out that the same problems are encountered when no hiding is involved.

Figure 6-1 shows the tasks that mark advance through the stages of the object concept. As can be seen, hiding is not critical. (Indeed, hiding per se is no problem at all, for babies in stage II of the object concept will readily find an object that has been hidden by plunging the whole room into darkness, so that object, baby, and all are "out of sight.") The main problems in the tasks from stage III on can be described as problems centered on the *spatial relations between objects*. it is objects on, in, under, behind, in front of, other objects that trouble the baby (see e.g., Wishart and Bower, 1984).

Piaget's original observations were of his own three children who were, of course, seen longitudinally. There have been few other long-term longitudinal studies (Wishart and Bower, 1984). Most studies have focused on one or the other transition, in particular the transition from stage IV to stage V, the place error. Theories of each transition have abounded, to the extent that many scientists doubt whether there is much sense in discussing the whole complex as the development of *the* object concept; perhaps there is no unitary underlying process beneath the surface skills, perhaps the object concept is merely a set of independent skills, acquired normally but not necessarily in the order of Figure 6-1. It is very difficult to show that any different behaviors are developmentally connected (Bower, 1974). We cannot follow embryologists, who can delete a supposed ancestor cell, reasoning from the nonappearance of the supposed descendent organs that there is a developmental link (see e.g., Spemann, 1938). We may find such links by accident in the study of handicap, as did Fraiberg (1964) with her finding that blind children who could not reach could not walk, whereas if they were taught to reach, they would walk as well, more or less immediately. The opportunity for such findings is, fortunately, rare. Instead we must turn to acceleration procedures (Bower, 1974, 1982). In this case we have two behavioral skills that appear at separate points in development. If the earlier occurring one is practiced to a peak not normally seen, we can look to see whether the later skill is accelerated in its appearance. Such acceleration is prima facie evidence for a link. I am aware that this argument is far from watertight.

Nonetheless I began, some years ago, a series of studies of acceleration of the behaviors that make up the object concept, a series that is not yet complete. In the first study (Bower and Paterson, 1972) babies were shown a simple tracking display in which an object moved from place to place, with occasional stops. The babies were twelve weeks old at the beginning of the study. Tracking experience was given weekly for 10 minutes a week, for 9 weeks. This very minimal addition to the babies' normal experience produced significant acceleration, extending even to the complex stage VI tasks.

The acceleration obtained in that study was most certainly not mediated by training in specific behavioral skills. I presume that the initial errors shown are determined by a particular idea of objects. The simplified tracking situation allows for correction of that initial idea, so that all of the baby's subsequent experience is interpreted in the light of the new, improved idea of objects. The most striking acceleration in the study was at the very beginning, with all of the babies very rapidly dropping nonfunctional responses from their repertoire. The rapidity of this change was presumably a function of the stark simplicity of the display, which lacked the distractions that would normally accompany moving objects.

The idea of correction being easier in a very stripped-down situation led to the next study. There the display featured one moving and stopping object and one of the three stationary objects (As shown on the right in Figure 6-1, p. 98). The display thus presented the baby with a spatial relations problem in addition to the problems posed by a straightforward moving object. Weekly tracking sessions were begun when the babies were twelve weeks old. The results in terms of acceleration were indeed dramatic. Virtually as soon as the babies became capable of manual search, they passed all of the tasks presented up to and including the stage V tasks. Stage VI tasks were likewise passed with very little delay. In terms of conventional measures Piaget's stages III and IV disappeared, the infants on manual search tasks going straight to stage V.

Close examination of all the data reinforced a formulation of the development of the object concept as a process in which three advances occur, the advances being necessarily sequential, each being

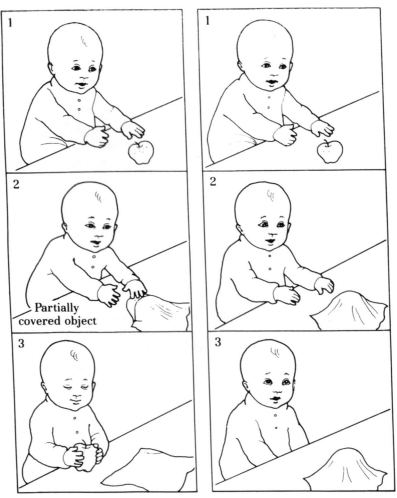

A stage III infant will reach out and take a partially
covered object (left), but he is unable to obtain an object that
has been completely covered by a cloth (right).

Figure 6-1 The behaviors that mark development of the object concept, stages
III through V. (From Bower, 1974, 1982.)

logically necessary for its successor. The model assumes that from
birth the child, like the adult, defines an object as a bounded volume
of space. I further assume that from a very early age, perhaps birth
(Slater et al., 1985) the baby identifies a stationary object with its
place and a moving object with its path of movement. Thus if the
baby is presented with a stationary object which then moves to a new
place, the baby will continue to look to the old place for the object.

The stage IV infant thinks that an object that has been
hidden will always be found at the same place.
(Photographs by Jennifer Wishart.)

Figure 6-1 (*continued*)

Similarly if the baby is presented with a moving object that stops, the
baby will search for the moving object along its prior path of movement. At this stage, the transformation of a stationary object in its

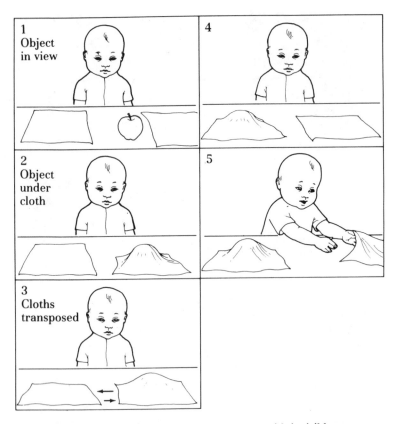

The stage V infant cannot yet cope with invisible displacements of the object.

Figure 6-1 *(continued)*

place will not result in search for the now unseen, untransformed object (for more detailed reviews, see Bower 1971, 1974, 1982).

The first advance occurs whenever the baby redefines an object as a bounded volume of space that can move from place to place. At a stroke, the errors touched on above will disappear. However, the baby still has no way of dealing with spatial relations; the moment one object is placed on another, the baby's definition of an object will tell him or her that both objects have gone, replaced by a new object defined by the spatial boundary of the pair. It is boundary loss that causes confusions; an object in front of or behind another poses no problems, unless the objects are in contact, sharing — and losing — a boundary (Schonen and Bower, 1978). Before the baby can cope with any of the problems posed by the tasks shown under stages III, IV, and V of Figure 6-1, he or she must reformulate his or her

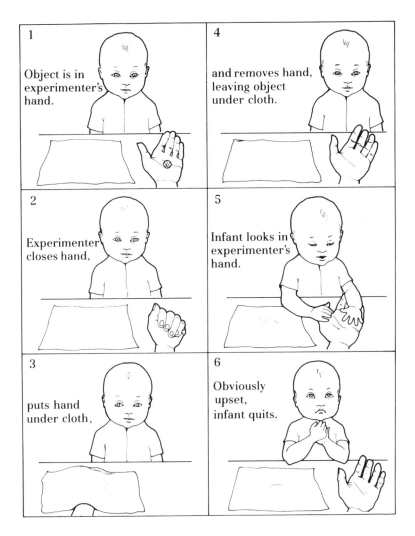

1	4
Object is in experimenter's hand.	and removes hand, leaving object under cloth.
2	5
Experimenter closes hand,	Infant looks in experimenter's hand.
3	6
puts hand under cloth,	Obviously upset, infant quits.

The stage V infant is also unable to infer that, if the object is not in the experimenter's hand, it must be under the cloth.

Figure 6-1 (*continued*)

definition of an object, adding to it the corollary that two objects can share a common boundary without either losing its own identity. As has been shown (pp. 83–85), the baby with this definition of an object will still have problems with stage VI tasks. To solve them, the baby must define an object as a bound volume of space that can move from place to place, contacting other objects and *sharing their movement under some circumstances*. It is probably the "some" above that makes this advance come so late and with considerable difficulty.

This outline of the development of the object concept can be made very precise, precise enough that a computer program of the description can stimulate the behavior of infants in object concept tasks (Luger et al., 1983).

I would like to elaborate on the developmental model described above, relating it to the ideas outlined in Chapter 2. In Chapter 2 I argued that the perceptual system of the young infant is more abstract and less differentiated than that of the adult. The account of the object concept given above grew up with and out of these notions. It assumes that an infant defines an object as a volume of space bounded in three dimensions. This is a simple definition and does not seem at odds with the definition that operates within the adult perceptual system (Michotte, Thines and Crabbe', 1964). However, I am also assuming that the young infant uses much simpler, less differentiated ways to identify an object than does the adult. I maintain that the infant does identify objects, that he or she reaches decisions that one object is the same object over time or space and that another object is a different object. We adults have complicated rules for identification, rules which can be suspended on occasion, leaving us, I suspect, in a similar state as the infant (Michotte, et al., op. cit.).

I have proposed two early rules for identification. "An object is the same object if it is in the same place" is one. "An object is the same object if it is on the same path of movement" is the other. These two rules can account for the kind of odd behavior first described by Piaget in *The Child's Construction of Reality* (1955). Suppose one presents an infant with a stationary object in place A; while the infant is looking, set the object in motion so that it moves to place B. What kind of behavior does this elicit? The infant will track the object from A to B, comprehensibly enough. However, the infant will also look along the extension of the path of the movement defined by A to B. These extensions of accommodation," as Piaget called them, would result if the baby were looking for the object defined by the path of the movement. The behavior looks odd to us because we know that the object that was on that path of movement is safely stationary at B. However, a system like that of the infant, or that I have ascribed to the infant, would not produce any such conclusion. The infant should look at the stationary object at B, but should also look for the now

102

vanished moving object that had been seen between A and B. Indeed, the infant should look back to A to see what has happened to the object there, and this does indeed occur. These behaviors look odd to us, but they are not at all odd; indeed, they are wholly predictable, given the definition of identity outlined above.

Overcoming these errors is the first step down the path that leads to development of the object concept. It is a step that can be accelerated and we can, in a way, see why the step is made. We adults present the baby with an object at A which we then move to B. For us there is one object involved. The baby, by contrast, acts as if there were three objects involved: the object at A, the object at B, and the object on the path A B. If we then move the object back to A, we increase the number of objects in the baby's world to four: the object at A, the object at B, the moving object on the path A B, and another moving object on the path B A. The infant's world will be greatly simplified by complicating his or her criteria for identity so that the situation described here is seen as involving only one object. A reduction from four to one is a significant gain for the baby, bought at the cost of a more complex identification rule.

I had and still have some hope of attaching numbers to cost and gain. If we view the infant as a computer making decisions there is a cost in the processing space it takes to impose more complex identification rules. There is equally a gain in the reduction of the number of objects whose fate must be stored; in the case above, a reduction of three. Unfortunately, the modeling work mentioned above is not yet advanced enough for precise numbers to be available. However, the modeling work has one important conceptual benefit that I must mention, although it is somewhat aside from the main line of this discussion. In elaborating the computer model of infant functioning, I described in words what I thought the baby saw in a situation. The baby's percepts and rules went from me to the computer scientist as sentences in English. The sentences were translated into a computer language PROLOG. My representation of the baby's world was given in propositional sentences. The computer's representation was likewise propositional. The outcome was that the computer could mimic the behavior of a baby. It thus seems to be that it is fair for us to represent what goes on in the mind of a child by sentences in English. I do not think for a moment that babies think in English, much less my version of it, but I do think that their thought is propositional, and that it can be represented by sentences in English.

Acceleration of this simple first step of the object concept can accelerate success in later stages, stages involving tasks that cannot even be presented until months later. How is this possible? Again, to understand it I think we must accept that the perceptual system and therefore the learning of the young infant is more general and less specific than that of the adult. In the acceleration situation the infant is presented with an object. Despite this, the infant learns about all objects, or so I would argue. It is only the generality that makes acceleration possible.

We thus have a very rich picture of the development of the object concept. We can describe behavior in behavioral terms, we can do it at one step removed and with sufficient precision that a computer can comprehend what we have done and repredict behavior, and we have enough insight into the process that we can produce massive developmental gains. And yet can we truly say that we have an explanation of the development of the object concept? I think there are two things missing. One is an account of why we get the peculiar but systematic pattern of errors that we do. For the moment I would like to look at the primary question: why does development occur?

This question is not often asked, presumably because in the context of normal development, the answer seems obvious. Developmental changes help us function more adequately in the real world, and so are clearly a "good thing" from the point of view of evolutionary theory or behavior theory. Since I would like a theory of development to account for abnormal and normal development, I can scarcely find this line of reasoning satisfactory. I am also not even sure that it is valid in the context of the object concept. There are many organisms that seem perfectly well adjusted to the "real" world, without having anything at all like the mature object concept of the human infant (e.g., Gruber, 1971; Etienne, 1972).

Any thinking about why the baby develops an object concept could as well begin with an analysis of why babies will sit for hour after hour, week after week, going through the various little tests we give them. It is quite clearly not because they want the toy that is hidden. It is highly unlikely that they have any interest in the toy per se, and it is surely obvious that they have more direct resources available to get that toy or any other toy that really interests them. Attaining the toy consistently is only a signal that they have understood the whole problem situation, a signal to them as much as a signal to us. But what is it that signals to them that there is something to be understood? What is their measure of understanding? In a lab situation it can be 100 percent success, but never that, surely, in the real world. The lab situation is the real world purified, but there are sufficient differences that we must surely postulate some process other than extrinsic success to signal comprehension to the baby, and some process other than extrinsic failure to signal that there is something to be understood.

Let us return to a simple tracking situation in which an object moves repetitively from place to place, pausing at each of the two places. As we have noted, an infant who does not understand what is going on here can cope with the problem at a functional level, keeping his or her eyes on the object as he or she wishes, looking off, catching it again, and so on. Where is the problem? If we look at the situation as a set of "$\rightarrow$" equations, I think we can see that there is no problem. If we let A = place 1, B = place 2, L = leftward movement path, and R = rightward movement path, we can describe the baby's understanding as shown by his or her search rules, as

1. $-A \rightarrow (B \lor L \lor R)$ i.e., if there is nothing at A, there will be something at B or L or R

2. $-B \rightarrow (A \lor L \lor R)$

3. $-L \rightarrow (A \lor B \lor R)$

4. $-R \rightarrow (A \lor B \lor L)$

This does describe the baby's state of understanding. Babies at this stage, remember, are not puzzled by the sudden—to our eyes impossible—appearance of the object in two places at once. The only thing that puzzles them is the appearance of the object outside that domain. Why then should there be any development? For simplicity's sake, let us look at still younger infants, like those described by Bullinger (1977), who in this situation ignore movement and attend only to place. Their knowledge is

1. $-A \rightarrow B$ if there is nothing at A, there will be something at B

2. $-B \rightarrow A$

Let us look at the truth table for these equations, each of which, of course, is the *modus tollens* version of the other:

A	B	$-A \rightarrow B$	$-B \rightarrow A$
true	true	true	true
false	true	true	true
true	false	true	true
false	false	false	false

Both of these equations predict the same set of conjunctions, $-A.B$, $A.-B$ and $A.B$.

Even very young infants do test for this last conjunction, looking between where the object is and where it was. They never find it in both locations.

Now let us return to our more sophisticated baby with four loci of search. This baby must expect simultaneous appearance of the object in two, three, or four locations. To say that the search for such conjunctions becomes an obsession in fifteen- to sixteen-week-olds is hardly an exaggeration. I have seen one protocol in which no less than 84 off-object looks occurred in the course of one to-and-from movement of the object. Such conjunctions of appearances never occur, and the only conclusion the baby can come to is that the overall hypothesis or set of hypotheses guiding his or her behavior is seriously flawed. However, by this time, processes of perceptual development will mean that the baby is registering not just place and movement but also size, shape, color, etc. Up to this point the baby knows that he or she can find his or her bounded volume in two places, A or B, or on two movement paths, L or R. To summarize, he or she knows $A \vee B \vee L \vee R$. Given perceptual development, the baby will be registering featural information, F, as well. The baby thus knows: $AF \vee BF \vee LF \vee RF$. The simplest logical reduction device will instantly change this to $F(A \vee B \vee L \vee R)$ which would read in ordinary language as "there is an object, F, that can move between A and B." In other words, the discovery of the object follows from the application of a simple logical principle to the information given. Because the information in the laboratory situation is clean and pure, the relevance of the principle can be more readily seen, hence the acceleration one can obtain with laboratory experience. Regrettably, the exposure prior to perceptual development should produce only disgust with the whole situation and hence a slowing of development, if anything. I did one such study and did produce that unhappy result, fortunately a temporary effect (Bower, 1974, 1982).

In terms of the specific "errors" one sees in this kind of situation, they surely reflect hypothesis testing, and are signs of a systematic intelligence at work. What then is this systematic intelligence doing? At the beginning it was theorized that objects may be identified in terms of place or movement, but not both, and not by any other means. We present the baby with a simple tracking situation. The baby searches for just one glimpse of all four objects at once, and does not succeed. (Wishart and I have attempted a study in which the baby would have succeeded, predicting that this odd event would satisfy the baby and reduce the frequency of looking at the display. The data are, in the main, still unanalyzed; however, preliminary analyses are not at all discouraging.) In the real world it would seem to me, the nonoccurrence of predicted objects must weaken the validity of the theories that generate the prediction. The theories predict in the situation that the baby will see one, two, three, or four objects; the baby can never see more than one. The nonoccurrence of the two, three, or four objects will not falsify the theories but might be enough to give them the valuation *neither true nor false*, which is to say, irrelevant. The view of the world which incorporates these theories is not, remember, lost; it can be reawakened in adults (Michotte, op. cit.).

Growth in the perceptual system plus a very simple logical mechanism would, as we have seen, produce an alternative and more adequate theory, a theory which can be readily confirmed. If the infant now defines an object as a bounded volume of space that can move from place to place, identified by sensory features, the baby will predict that only one object will be seen in our simple tracking situation, a prediction that is readily fulfilled. This kind of prediction will be susceptible to confirmation at all times. A violation would surely upset the baby. One simple violation that can be done with mirrors is to present the baby with multiple versions of a truly unique object, his or her mother (Figure 6-2). This does upset older babies, at least for a short time. The essence of the description being offered here is that it asserts that the baby formulates hypotheses and tests and modifies them on rational principles.

Very similar considerations apply to the second great advance of object concept development. The baby's problem here, recall, is that he or she does not realize that two objects can go into spatial relation

Figure 6-2 Multiple "mothers." A very simple optical arrangement, using mirrors, allows one to present infants with multiple images of a unique object. (From Bower, 1979.)

and still exist as separate objects; two objects in relation are seen as a new object. Let us call the objects A and B and the new object C. The baby will probably notice that whenever A and B are present, C is not, i.e., in a simple tracking situation. A would be the small cube, B the platform and C the cube-on-platform. Symbolically this can be written: $A.B \rightarrow -C$, and vice versa $C \rightarrow -A.-B$. In ordinary language: "whenever there is a cube and a platform, there is no cube-on-platform; whenever there is a cube-on-platform, there is no cube and no platform." Working out the truth table for these equations gives a set of possible conjunctions (Table 6-1). Babies do test these conjunctions, producing patterns of looking behavior that are "illogical" if maintaining contact with an object is the aim, but perfectly logical if the purpose is testing two logical hypotheses.

However, a closer examination of the predicted conjunctions reveals an anomaly. The equations given above involve three events: the seeing of a cube (A), the seeing of a platform (B), and the seeing of a cube-on-platform (C). Whenever the cube (A) and the platform (B) are seen $(A.B)$, the cube-on-platform (C) is not seen $(-C)$. Adopting our usual shorthand we have:

$$A.B \rightarrow -C$$

Table 6-1 Truth table for tracking situation

Hypothesis	$A.B \rightarrow -C$	$C \rightarrow -A.-B$
Predicted	$A.B.-C$	$-A.-B.-C$
	$A.-B.-C$	$A.-B.-C$
	$-A.B.-C$	$-A.B.-C$
Conjunction to be seen simultaneously	$-A.B.C.$	$-A-B.C$
	$A-B.C$	$A.-B.-C$
	$-A.-B.C.$	$A.B.-C$

Likewise whenever the cube-on-platform is seen, C, the cube is not seen, $-A$, and the platform is not seen, $-B$. This gives us:

$$C \rightarrow -A.-B$$

Now if we look through the possible occurrences of all three events (Table 6-1), we will see that C is predicted to occur under a variety of circumstances; in particular it can, indeed must, occur whenever neither the cube nor the platform are visible, $-A.-B$. However, it can also occur, is predicted to occur, whenever the cube and the platform are not seen simultaneously, $-(A.B)$. Now the events $-A.-B$ and $-(A.B)$ are not equivalent, as their ordinary language equivalents make clear. $-A.-B$ is equivalent to saying that neither A nor B can be seen; $-(A.B)$ is equivalent to saying that either A or B cannot be seen.

There are clearly possible circumstances in which one could assert that $-A.-B$ was false while asserting that $-(A.B)$ is true. It is here that the anomaly arises. C can occur when $-A.-B$ is true and also, in principle, at least, when $-A.-B$ is false. This is clearly anomalous. I have been arguing that infants can evaluate relations between events in a four-valued space. However, events exist only in a two-valued space; they either occur or they do not occur. C is an event. It cannot both occur and not occur, as logic would lead one to assume on the hypothesis given above. By thinking through the sequence above, the baby can discover that he or she is hypothesizing about an unreal event.

Now C is an event. If it must have an unreal value, then it does not happen, does not exist. This discovery is the solution to this object concept problem. The substitution of real events for C will follow. C will be differentiated into A, B, and a spatial relation. The discovery of all spatial relations will take time. The initial step is the important one. It follows from casting what is given in a logical form, and deducing the consequences. I have argued that development can proceed simply as a result of the baby *thinking*. Normally the baby will be given information that will lead him or her to conclude that *C* is unreal. However, the information can be pretty minimal. I am thinking here of limbless infants studied by Gouin-Décarie (1969) who managed to pass along the stages of the object concept at a pretty normal rate, despite having to do without a vast amount of normally available information. The important part of the development is internal; it is a change in the construal of the information given. Such a change cannot result from the information given but only by "thinking through." Acceleration will again result from presentation of pure, simple givens, allowing the problem to be cast and solved by the built-in computing system of the child. In the real world, the casting of the problem will take more time, simply because the information does not come in such a clean, pure form. The solution to the problem, though, is internal, resulting from working out the consequences of hypotheses derived from the information given.

The internal changes produced by acceleration experiments can produce pretty massive gains in the rate of development of the object concept (Wishart and Bower, 1985). In essence, that study found that the stage IV error, the place error, the most studied component of the object concept sequence, could be deleted from the developmental process. On my own theory of what is happening in the development of the object concept, that is not surprising. The information required to succeed in these tasks can be given before manual search is possible. If the information is used, the problem will be solved by the time manual search is possible, so that manual search will not exhibit either the stage III or the stage IV error. I should emphasize that Wishart and Bower (op. cit.) was a blind study. Both authors expected some acceleration but not the massive effects that were found. The testers were not preset to elicit these results — indeed were puzzled by the results. Nonetheless the results obtained were pretty impressive, particularly in view of the difference between the training and the test situation. In the training situation the babies looked at an object moving backward and forward from place to place, passing on top of, or through, or behind another object (Figure 6-3). The test situation was a straight manual testing situation with a stationary object with cups placed on top of it. Formally

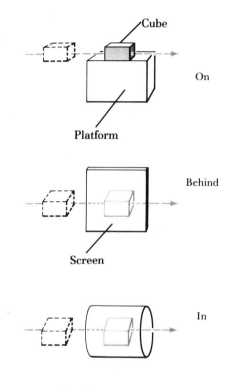

Tunnel

Figure 6-3 In a simple tracking task, in the training situation, the baby sees an object move from place to place, for part of its movement in contact with another stationary object. (Adapted from Bower 1974, 1982.)

both involve the same spatial relations; at the sensory level they are very different indeed. Transfer is further evidence of the general, abstract nature of the infant's construal system, very different indeed from the sensory particulars we would pick up in the same situation.

I asked Dr. Wishart to do a further experiment to attempt in essence to ruin the acceleration (Wishart, 1979). The rationale for the second experiment was as follows: the acceleration seen in the previous experiment depended on the child forming an abstract representation of what was going on in the tracking, abstract enough that it could transfer to the very different looking manual search tasks; the training phase involved the baby looking at three different spatial relations, each for a relatively brief period. What would happen if the training period concentrated on a single relation? It is

111

at least possible that the training period would change the child's construal of what is going on in the tracking task to something that was too specific to transfer immediately to the manual tasks. The baby could have formulated a description of what was going on in the tracking task that was so detailed that there was no connection to be made with the manual search task, and hence acceleration should have been minimized.

These results are not as impressive as they might be. However, please keep them in mind because they may point us in the direction of a corrective technique that could be applied to early abstract acquisitions that are having adverse effects: perceptual differentiation might prevent premature generalization of some early hypotheses.

What of actual performance on object concept tasks? Is there a logic to the seeming illogical behavior? Some logical ideas and their application have already been sketched out. The most ambitious essay is by Barry Richards (1985) who has tried to explain performance in the stage IV or place error task. The analysis that follows differs from his in major ways but would not have been possible without his efforts.

The task whose failure indicates stage IV was shown in Figure 5-1. The baby is shown two cups and a toy. With the baby watching, the toy is hidden twice under one cup (A) and then under the other cup (B). On this third trial, typically the baby picks up cup A and ignores cup B, even after finding nothing under A. To understand this, let us consider again some ideas of relevance logic, ideas that were initially espoused in a psychological context by Piaget (1981). Relevance logic asserts that any proposition may be assigned one of four truth values. The truth values and their interrelations were shown in Figure 4-6. "Value" diminishes from top to bottom in the figure. The two intermediate values, *both true and false* and *neither true nor false*, are equivalent but incommensurable. Value is important in that a proposition may imply another proposition only if the former is of the same or lower value than the latter. However, no implication is possible between the two intermediate values since they are incommensurable. Thus a proposition that is *both true and false* cannot imply a statement that is *neither true nor false*. The arrows in Figure 4-6 indicate the truth value of the negation of the proposition that has a given truth value. As can be seen there, there is no change with the intermediate truth values.

This is all familiar and has been rehearsed in previous chapters. I must now add some details about the effect on the evaluation of an hypothesis of successive instances of it. The instances may have different values from one another and from the hypothesis. An instance, I have insisted, is an event in the world; it either happens or it does not. An instance is thus either true or false. An hypothesis, by contrast, makes a general statement about the world which can take on any of the four values of the lattice. There is a kind of logical arithmetic that decides how one combines values (Mackinson, 1973). To that I wish to add some psychology. Specifically, I want to assume that the baby keeps some kind of running record of instances of an hypothesis in mind, along with a general evaluation of the hypothesis, trying to combine them into a consonant general evaluation. Thus suppose the baby has an hypothesis. The hypothesis is tested and, on that instance, the baby finds the hypothesis true. The baby could conclude the hypothesis was true. Suppose, on the next instance, the baby finds the hypothesis does not predict what happens, that instance indicating that the hypothesis was false. The baby with a four-valued logical system could conclude that the hypothesis was *both* true and false. That would be in accord with the logical arithmetic.

Suppose, though, the baby begins with an hypothesis that the baby believes to be *neither true nor false*. That is not impossible; indeed it is likely that the baby would so evaluate an hypothesis which had not been tested. Now suppose the baby tests the hypothesis and finds an instance in which the prediction from the hypothesis is true. If the baby applies the logical arithmetic to his initial valuation and the value of the instance, he will still evaluate the hypothesis as neither true nor false. That is the way the arithmetic works. Suppose the next application of the hypothesis shows it, in that instance, to be false. The baby will thus have in mind for that hypothesis that it is *neither true nor false, true* and *false*. The latter two will add up to give *both true and false*. Summing that with *neither true nor false*, on the logical rules, leads to an outcome value, *false*. This is one way in which the valuation *neither true nor false* can change.

What has all of this to do with the object concept? To get to baby behavior we have to make certain assumptions. The first of these is that the baby's behavior is the outcome of rational thought process, processes that could be described by relevance or some other logic. This assumption is not as heterodox as it might once have seemed.

The second assumption is that the baby at stage IV does not understand what is going on in object concept testing. This is hardly controversial, given that there are many other tasks the child must pass after the stage IV task before it could be said that he or she understood the object concept. The last assumption is that babies at this stage of development attempt to compress all of the information given about an object or event into a single general proposition about the object or event. This does seem to be a general characteristic of the infant cognitive system (Bower, 1974, 1982).

Given these assumptions, what is the baby to make of the stage IV task? The baby sees two cups A and B. His or her attention is drawn to one of them (A) by the hiding event. He or she picks up A and finds a toy. On the second trial the same thing happens. What will the infant know at this point in the experiment? We would say that the infant's knowledge can be summarized in two propositions with association truth values. These are

1. It is *true* that there is a toy under cup A.

2. It is *neither true nor false* that there is a toy under cup B.

Proposition 1 accords with everything the baby knows about cup A. Proposition 2 accords with everything the baby knows about cup B and toys, which is effectively, nothing.

What will happen on the catch trial when the toy is hidden under cup B? The baby does not understand the hiding event. If he or she wants the toy, he or she will deduce from what he knows that he or she should pick up cup A. When the baby does so, he or she will discover that there is no toy there. As the baby absorbs this information, what will happen? First, the baby will have to change his or her evaluation of proposition 1 above to

3. It is *both true and false* that there is a toy under cup A.

Second, the baby will be unable to go to cup B. The baby's task looks simple. He or she is faced with a choice between A and B; ($A \lor B$) and he or she knows that there is no toy under A ($-A$). The baby must thus reason through a disjunctive syllogism:

$$A \vee B$$
$$-A$$
$$\therefore B$$

This can also be written as $(A \vee B).-A \rightarrow B$. However, A is now assigned the value *both true and false*, which means that $-A$ has the same value, while B has the value *neither true nor false*. $A \vee B$ is *true* in logic, but the conjunction $(A \vee B).-A$ is *both true and false*. Recall that no implication is possible between such incommensurable statements. The baby, having made the error, is stuck, unable to correct. This is an accurate account of what happens in conventional tests.

What will happen after that? In repeated tests of the form $AABBBA$, etc., we can assume that the baby will eventually pick up B when there is a toy underneath it. This will not change the child's evaluation of the proposition "there is a toy under cup B." If the child composes the presentation where it was true that there was a toy under cup B with the presentations where the proposition was *neither true nor false*, the value will remain at the lower point. The child will thus once more be unable to correct on a catch trial, like trial 6 of the sequence outlined above. However, the discovery that there is no toy under B will change the evaluation of the proposition about B. Successively the child has been given (i) no information about whether there is or is not a toy under B, (ii) information that there is a toy under B, and (iii) information that there is no toy under B. The composition of (ii) and (iii) will give the value *both true and false*. *Both true and false*, and *neither true nor false*, are incommensurable and cannot be combined, save into a lower value, *false*. However long the evaluation takes, the child should end up with the value *false* for the proposition "there is a toy under cup B." This has the immense advantage that the child can go straight to A. The implication $(A \vee B).-B \rightarrow A$ is fine since $-B$ — *false* — has a lower value than A — *both true and false*.

The discovery of a toy under A will not change the evaluation of A; the proposition that there is a toy under A will retain the *both true and false* value. What then will happen on the ninth trial when the toy is really under B? The baby will discover no toy under A but will really be trapped, since $-A$ with its both *true and false* value cannot imply B; the proposition that there is a toy under B has a *false* value, and a proposition of a given value cannot imply a proposition of a lower value, and reference back to Figure 5-1 will show that *false* is the lowest value.

We must presume that eventually the baby will pick up *B*, and discover that there is a toy under it. This will change the value of the proposition "there is a toy under *B*" to *both true and false*. *A* and *B* will thus have the same value and the baby should have no further trouble in following through the disjunctive syllogism to correct any errors. However, at this stage the baby should have no reason to choose one cup rather than another, since both have the same value. This 50/50 choice probability is characteristic of infant behavior on catch trials, the *B* trials in an *AAB* sequence, over a long series of trials (Bower and Patterson, 1972). On the analysis presented here, 50/50 choices should also occur on non-catch trials. Unfortunately for this account, experimenters do not typically allow this to happen; the baby must get two *A* trials right to be presented with a *B* trial. One exception was a study by de Schonen and Bower (1978) which allowed babies to respond as they wished on *A* trials. Over a series of alternating presentations of the form (*AABBA* . . .), they found that error was as likely in non-catch trials as in catch trials, in the later trial blocks of the series. At the time, this result seemed odd and we could not explain it, or give any account of it save in terms of boredom. It does fit with the logical analysis presented here.

The most direct test of the account offered here would probably be to take latency of response measures over a series of trials. The account offered here makes clear predictions of latency differences as the child progresses through a series of trials.

A test of these predictions would not be as easy as it might seem. A perfectly naive baby should go through the sequence outlined above. Few babies, in Edinburgh at least, come naive to these tests. Not all these babies go through this stage of development (Wishart and Bower, 1985). Partly for that reason it seemed worthwhile to attempt a more direct test of the assumptions underlying this account. These assumptions are

1. That babies will assign one of four truth values to a proposition about an object of event;

2. the value assigned will incorporate all of the information given about the object or event; and

3. where no information is given, any proposition will have the value *neither true nor false.*

Four slightly different tasks, all involving choice between two cups, were given. Each task consisted of four presentation trials and one search trial. On each presentation trial the infant saw one or both of the cups lifted up, either revealing a toy or revealing nothing. The schedule of presentations is given in Table 6-2. At the end of each block of four presentation trials, the infant was given a search trial in which he or she was allowed to lift up the cups to find the toy him or herself. On the first two presentations, there was a toy under both cups; on the second pair, there was no toy under either cup.

All four search trials involved choice between two cups, with the possibility of correction. Presentation series I gives the child information that the proposition "there is a toy under cup A" (A) is *neither true nor false,* while the proposition "there is a toy under cup B" (B) is *both true and false.* Series IV gives the same outcome from a logical point of view, with A being *neither true nor false,* and B being *both true and false.* The evaluation of A in both of these seems

Table 6-2 Schedule of presentation for tasks 1, 2, 3, and 4

	Presentation							
	I		II		III		IV	
Cup	A	B	A	B	A	B	A	B
Trial								
1	0	+	+	+	+	−	0	+
2	+	−	+	−	−	+	+	−
3	0	+	−	+	−	−	+	+
4	+	−	−	−	+	+	0	−

Note: 0 = the cup is touched but not lifted; + = the cup is lifted to reveal a toy; − = the cup is lifted to reveal nothing.

counterintuitive but it is clearly the only one which includes all of the information given about A. Logic gives us no guide as to whether the child will go to A or to B; however, it does predict that there will be no search of whichever is the second cup. It is clear here that any "common sense" approach to infants would make very different predictions. Since the child has twice seen a toy at A and has never seen nothing at A, common sense would clearly predict an initial choice of A. Lack of an object at A in IV should then trigger a rapid search at B. Series II and III are designed to give a choice between A and B where both have truth values of *both true and false*. In neither case is there a logical reason for a delayed second search. Presentations I and II both incorporate information that there are two objects available, hence information for a second search after retrieval of a toy from under whichever cup is chosen first.

The study outlined here was designed to discover whether or not these logical considerations played any part in object concept performance. An unusual feature of the study was that it was done as part of a practical course for third-year undergraduates, with the undergraduates serving as experimenters. Among the other obvious advantages of this procedure is the possibility of avoiding experimenter bias. Object permanence testing is very social. Both mother and baby can be given information about what the experimenter expects them to do; this could create artifacts, artifacts that can only be avoided by using experimenters who have no expectations. Naive experimenters can be as important as naive subjects.

One-hundred-thirty third-year psychology students served as experimenters. They had been introduced to conventional object permanence tests with videotapes. They had been advised to read Piaget (1955) or, as a secondary source, Bower (1977) or Bower (1982). They were divided into groups of three and given the following instructions:

> In this practical, you will be examining the baby's ability on a variety of object concept tasks. In all tasks the baby will be presented with a toy or toys that are to be found. If the baby seems bored or uncooperative, you may use a new toy. With the mother's permission you may substitute chocolate or raisins for the toys, if the baby is uncooperative. On all search trials ask the mother to hold the baby's arms until you have withdrawn your hands and sat back. This should take one second at

least. After one further second tell the mother to let the baby go. There are three tasks. Each student should present one task. The three tasks will all involve two cups referred to hereafter as *A* and *B*. In your group *A* is the cup on your *right*/left. Your group will do the tasks in the order — — —

In all tasks allow the baby 60 seconds to make an initial response, then allow another 60 seconds for another response.

Task 1 is the stage IV/V transition task. Place a toy on the table between two cups. Pick up both cups and place them on the table so that cup *A* conceals the toy. Push the cups toward the baby until both are in reach but are the width of the baby's shoulders apart. Remove your hands, sit back and tell the mother to release her baby. There are 12 trials of this task; the concealing cup will be on each trial:

$$A\,A\,B\,B\,B\,A\,A\,A\,B\,B\,B\,A$$

Task 2 is the V/VI transition task. It begins as above. After the cups are in position, transpose them so that *A* is where *B* was, and vice versa. Present this task 6 times with the initial occluder. Use a different toy from task 1. The order of hiding is

$$A\,B\,B\,A\,A\,B$$

Between presentations 4 and 5 present a catch trial. Bring the cups down so that the toy is not occluded. Carry on as with the other trials, leaving the toy visible but unremarked.

In task 3 there are four search trials. Each search is preceded by four presentations where the baby looks but does not touch. On each sequence use a different pair of differently coloured cups. Between presentations, conceal what you are doing with a card. Presentation sequences are outlined below (see table 1). For each separate presentation sequence use a different toy or toys. Your presentation sequence is — — — —

The testing sequences were then demonstrated twice. The experimenters were monitored by myself and two demonstrators. Order of testing and side were specified for each group, so that for half, *A* was on the right, with order of testing counterbalanced over the group.

Forty-five babies between six and seventeen months of age served as subjects. They were brought in by their mothers or fathers, or both, who stayed with them at all times.

All behavior was recorded on videotape. After the testing was over, the experimenters recorded the latencies of response to cups in all presentations.

In tasks 1 and 2, a failure to respond after an initial error was assigned a latency of 60 seconds plus the latency of the first response. In task 3, all failures to give a second response were given the arbitrary latency of 60 seconds plus the latency of the first response. Each baby's latency scores were then converted to Z scores by the students themselves.

The basic results are set out in Figure 6-4. There was no effect of task order or gender. In conventional terms, no subject "passed" either task 1 or task 2. On the catch trial of task 2, only 6 infants went straight to the visible toy. The remainder picked up and inspected both cups before going for the toy.

The pattern of results does seem to support the idea that logical factors are involved in performance of some object concept tasks.

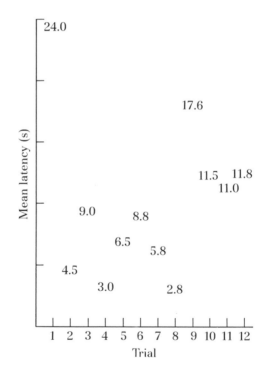

A

Figure 6-4 (A) Trial by trial latencies (in seconds) on task 1. (B) Proportion of correct first responses on task 1. (C) Latency (in seconds) of cup search in task 3.

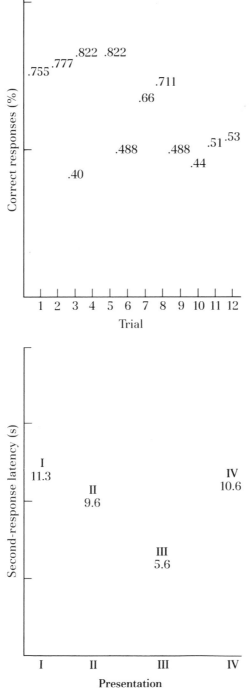

B

C

Clearly a small scale study of this kind is more than suggestive. Numerous controls would be required to pin down logic as the source of the pattern of responses found in task 3. One might ask whether the investment would be worthwhile. All that one would attain is proof that there is one more factor to add to the list of factors that affect performance on the stage IV/V transition task.

There is nothing in what we have said thus far to account for the eventual solution of the problems of the object concept. The infant, at this point, still does not understand what is going on in the task and has no way of producing correct responses at will. The baby should, as he or she does, choose on a random basis. The random choice can be seen as a systematic testing of a general hypothesis about the situation. The infant, we are supposing, believes that the propositions, (A) "There is a toy under cup A" and (B) "There is a toy under cup B," both have the value *both true and false*. The propositions both reflect general hypotheses about the task. On any given task presentation, there either is or is not a toy under A, and there either is or is not a toy under B. Furthermore, if there is a toy under A, there is not one under B. On any presentation, A is *true* and B is *false*, or vice versa. Over trials the baby never finds A and B both *true* or both *false*, as he might reasonably expect. The statement $A \lor B$ is always *true*, not sometimes *false*, as it would have to be to fit with the values assigned to A and B.

If our infant at this stage is testing for evidence to confirm his or her general hypotheses about A and B, then he or she will not find it. Furthermore, if the baby is formulating an hypothesis about A or B, he or she will discover a logical contradiction, for $A \lor B$ is always true, and always has been *true*, and that is incompatible with A.B having the value *both true and false*. These epistemic irritations could result in the baby formulating a new hypothesis summarized as: $(A \lor B).-(A.B)$. This reformulation is of the same order as those proposed to account for changes in the infant's understanding of objects, arising for much the same reasons (Bower, 1982; Luger, et al., 1983). This formulation would not amount to comprehension of the object concept, or even to the solution of this particular task. For the latter, the baby would have to formulate an hypothesis of the form: "In this task whenever an object vanishes mysteriously, (to find it) pick up the cup near which it was last seen."

This rule or hypothesis is not comprehension of the object concept, nor will it necessarily lead to correct performance. A baby using this rule and the reformulation outlined above could deliberately pick up the "wrong" cup to check that there was nothing there. Indeed, babies who seem to understand the task often do this.

To continue on this note, we should recall that a baby who had formulated this rule to cope with the IV/V transition tasks and who had had reinforcement for it might well do worse on higher-order tasks than a baby who had no such background, so that systematic testing on the IV/V task over a prolonged period could result in slowing of development.

As against all this gloom, I think it must be admitted that the logical reformulation offered above does add to our understanding of what is going on in object concept performance. Predicting a pattern of latency differences over 12 trials is no mean feat and does represent a theoretical advance. Everything that has been proposed is precise enough that it can be embodied in a computer model, and the resulting model will, I think, pass the Turing Test; that is, looking at behavior we will not be able to say whether it is generated by our computer or the baby.

What of the development of logic? Thus far we have been looking at the way logic could explain development in other areas. What of the logical mechanisms themselves? Do they change? The Piagetian insight was first to argue that infants are logical and rational, and second that they might use a logic that was unfamiliar to us. The object concept data shows that the baby retains an ability to shift between different systems of logic *using the logic that is appropriate to the information given.* Information is fitted into an hypothesis. That hypothesis is evaluated. If the evaluation is one that is irrelevant as a guide to action, this signals the baby to search for a new hypotheses. As we have seen in the object concept tasks, the baby eventually will do something, although it will take a while if there is no rational base for action. The action itself will have consequences, which will provide new information for new hypotheses and new evaluations. In this restless need to act is the source of freedom from the fetters of logic.

· · · ·
7

Social Development

In this chapter I would like to look at social development. The hypothesis that early experience plays a critical determining role in development is most strongly manifested in conventional interpretations of the social effects described in Chapter 1. Two main effects were described there. One of these, the effects of early gender labels, is possibly the most powerful developmental effect ever described; the early label, it is claimed, can override the effects of a whole chromosome. That effect by itself would be enough to shatter any idea that human development is merely the unfolding of a given genetic plan, as if the whole process were impervious to events in the psychological world.

The other class of effects is less dramatic. Bowlby (1951), reviewing a large literature on the effects of awful experiences on children, proposed that early happy interactions would buffer the child against any later insult that could be delivered by the adult world; the lack of such positive interactions, or a perversion in those interactions, could result in the child growing up as an affectional isolate, a psychopath even. Bowlby's ideas have always been controversial. Yet it is impossible for anyone to think of mounting replication studies. Bowlby reviewed work carried out in the aftermath of World War II, a time when there were thousands upon thousands of homeless, abandoned, orphaned children choking the streets and railway stations of Europe. There will never again, God willing, be such an opportunity for observation of these kinds of effects.

For less obvious reasons, I would not expect similar observations done now to produce similar results. I would not expect it because Bowlby has changed the world. The idea that infants need consistent affection as much as they need food is now a part of the psychological world of adults everywhere. It clearly was not, in the world before 1950. These ideas were revolutionary. They are now widely accepted, and at an implicit level, at all levels of care. I have occasion to go into hard-pressed and understaffed institutions dealing in the main with damaged infants. Amid all the stress and overwork, attention to the affectional needs of the infants is never abandoned. That would not have been true in the world before Bowlby. Institutional care itself is withering away, in most Western countries; it is necessary to make a very strong case before any child is committed to the best of and best intentioned of institutions.

Despite the widespread, almost unconscious acceptance of Bowlby's ideas, they remain as controversial now as when they were first penned. An unchanging point of contention is whether or not infants genuinely have social behaviors and social needs, or whether all of these are derived from supposedly more basic biological needs, such as the need for food and warmth. I would have thought that Spitz (1965) would have shown beyond doubt that infants have social needs. In this study there was a seriously raised death rate among infants whose biological needs were met but whose social needs were not. However, the doubts persist. Because no one would ever dream of replicating that study deliberately, speculations about diet and so on can spread unchecked. Part of the problem has been the lack of obvious social behavior in young infants. I use the phrase "social behavior" to denote any behavior directed at another human being and nothing else, the behavior being in no way a function of biological need, its exercise being its own reward. (For a lengthier discussion see Bower, 1979.) I had thought that there was one behavior that newborns demonstrated which was unambiguously social, the behavior labeled interactional synchrony (Sander and Condon, 1974).

The initial report was greeted with skepticism. I, myself, was a believer from the start partly because of my knowledge of and respect for the authors, partly because I could see the degree to which criticism had shaped the work that appeared in print. It is hard for me to see what hidden artifacts could have remained. The clincher for me was the demonstration of the effect in less than ideal circumstances, the filming of a television documentary. (BBC TV, 1976). Any behavior that emerges in those circumstances deserves our full attention.

I was all the more ready to believe the findings on interactional synchrony because some years before these data were published, I became familiar with the absence of interactional synchrony and the dire effects of its absence through a study by Stott (1962). Stott was actually attempting to work out the causal history of some instances of poor mother-infant relations, relations poor enough that the dread phrase "maternal deprivation" might be used. Stott found that in some such cases the mother, and therefore the baby, had been subjected to a degree of prenatal stress or preparuritional stress that would have led to miscarriage in the absence of medical intervention. The babies were, however, carried to term. Stott quotes the mother as saying that at birth they were not "cuddly" babies. One mother said to me of her son, "It's like holding a lump of wood." In this situation, as Stott pointed out, the mothers feel deprived, and a vicious circle of mutually depriving deprivation can soon be established. What the studies of interactional synchrony did for me were to define precisely what these mothers were missing and what thousands of mothers today are missing, for severe prenatal stress has not vanished from the world. We can intervene in this kind of cycle, and we could do more, if interactional synchrony is "cuddliness." I suppose that it is a healthy sign that the original findings are being challenged (rather than ignored). The more work there is, the sooner we will comprehend the behavior that is for me at least one of the earliest significant social behaviors.

The other highly visible social behavior that is seen in very young infants, less than one hour of age, is imitation. I have seen imitation and have known it occurs for a very long time. It is only recently that

127

I have been able to fit the behavior into my own general theoretical framework. The clue to the fit came from work on gender identity, so I will rapidly review the work that was critical to my understanding, work that in itself tells us something about social development.

In 1975 Lewis and Brooks published a study whose importance has not been fully realized, even yet. There are hundreds of studies of the perceptual abilities of young babies showing that the babies can do, albeit in simple or embryonic form, almost anything that an adult can do. The Lewis and Brooks study is the only unquestionable study to demonstrate that babies can do something that adults most definitely cannot do. What Lewis and Brooks did was to show babies pairs of projected slides, one showing a boy, one showing a girl aged around twelve months. The slides were shown to boy babies and girl babies of around the same age as the models. What the investigators found was that boy babies looked more at the slides of boy babies while the girl babies looked more at the slides of the girl babies.

This result has many interesting implications. The most astonishing is the most obvious, that babies can identify* the gender of other babies in static slide presentations. It is this ability that adults most signally lack. Over the last ten years I have amused myself by showing paired slides of boys and girls to various audiences. These audiences included perhaps 1,000 psychology students, 300 pediatric nurses, 100 pediatricians, 200 child psychologists, and 60 mothers of at least one boy and one girl. Not one of these adults has been able to identify the gender of the babies shown with consistency. By no measure, including, in desperation, preferential looking were any of these more or less sophisticated adults able to do what babies can do with ease.

So there we have our problem. Babies can do something that adults cannot do. How do they do it? What clues do they use to identify gender?

My first stab at an answer reflected my own introspections about how I would set about the task. Despite considerable experience with babies, I could think of no physiognomic or anatomic feature that would differentiate a clothed boy from a clothed girl. On the other

---

*I say "identify" rather than "discriminate" because the preferential looking is invariably directed toward the model of the same gender as the looker. Gender per se may not be involved but some kind of "like me" identification must inform the looking pattern.

hand, there are some clues that anyone could use that reflect differ- ences in the way we treat baby boys and baby girls in our society. For example, assuming that there is any hair at all, it is likely that girls will have longer hair than boys. Girls are conventionally dressed in lighter colors than boys — light pink or light yellow versus dark blue or dark brown, for example. Also, baby girls often wear dresses; nowadays boys never do. Their accessories too are socially biased. Baby girls very often have dolls; boys very rarely. Baby boys very often have drums or even toy weapons; baby girls very rarely have either. If all of these clues pointed in the same direction, one could guess with fair accuracy that one was looking at a boy, in one case, or a girl, in the other.

We therefore prepared a set of slides, showing the whole baby. All of the girls were dressed in a frilled dress and had a doll. All of the boys were dressed in dark blue dungarees and had a drum. Hair length was not systematically varied. (Mothers were unenthusiastic about us cutting their babies' hair, and the babies were unenthusias- tic about wearing wigs.)

The results were as one would expect; with a simultaneous presen- tation of a boy and a girl, boys looked significantly more at boys than at girls, and girls looked significantly more at girls than at boys.

We then did the experiment over again but this time with our models cross-dressed: the baby girls wore the dungarees and the baby boys wore the frilly dress. (Perhaps the most difficult thing in this whole series of experiments was inserting the baby boys into a frilly dress!) When the subjects viewed slides of these cross-dressed models, boys looked significantly more at the girls dressed up as boys and the girls looked significantly more at the boys dressed up as girls. In other words, there seemed to be no biologically based preference, rather a preference for the culturally normal accoutrements of the biology, an interesting enough result in itself in that it shows that by one year of age babies have picked up some of the conventions associated with gender in our culture. The same conventions deter- mined the judgments of adults; with these extreme presentations, adults and babies made the same identifications.

After the experiment was completed I had intended to let matters rest. However, alerted by these studies, I began to pay more attention to the social interactions of the babies in the waiting room of my laboratory. It is often the case that numbers of babies are there (with their mothers) waiting to be seen or waiting for a taxi home or just waiting while their mothers chat. Babies do interact socially from an early age. Interaction is most noticeable once the babies can crawl or walk. Given a choice, boys will associate with boys and girls will associate with girls. This looks like the pattern found in the slides.

However, it assuredly does not have the same basis. Baby girls, particularly those with an older brother, are often dressed in boys clothes, and this cross-dressing does not produce cross-association: boys do not find girls dressed as boys as socially attractive as real boys, while girls find girls dressed as boys more attractive than real boys. There is, of course, much more information available with real, solid, moving models than can ever be presented in a slide. A slide, or any photograph, is a frozen instant in time, a highly arti ficial stimulus, not at all biologically appropriate for testing a biological difference. Since the logistic difficulties of doing an experiment with real babies seemed insuperable, Aitken and I decided to make films of boy babies and girl babies, dressed appropriately or cross-dressed.

In all of the films the model began at the top right of the frame, walked diagonally to center frame, where there was a toy, a drum, or a doll. Girls and boys, when dressed as girls, walked to the doll. Girls and boys, when dressed as boys, walked to the drum. The models were encouraged to pick up the toy and play with it. All of the models then sat down. This was their own idea but was incorporated in the clips anyway. The resulting 30-second movies were shown in pairs to boy and girl subjects. Each pair presented comprised either an appropriately dressed girl with a doll and an appropriately dressed boy with a drum, or a cross-dressed girl with a drum and a cross-dressed boy with a doll.

The results showed quite clearly that movement can override culturally based clues to gender. The girl subjects looked more at the girl models, however they were dressed, and boy subjects looked more at the boy models however they were dressed. Within these overall results there were some interesting subresults. For example, boy subjects, presented with a cross-dressed boy and a cross-dressed girl, spent proportionately far more time looking at the boy than they did when presented with an appropriately dressed boy and an appropriately dressed girl. Their typical pattern of looking at the cross-dressed boy was a long stare, a glance off at nothing, followed by short looks, interspersed with looking off. It was almost as if the boys found the sight of a boy dressed in girls' clothes extremely puzzling, almost shocking. No such pattern was found with girls.

That result in effect reinstated our original problem. Babies can detect the gender of other (moving) babies, regardless of the clothes they are wearing and the toy they are playing with. Adults most signally cannot.

The results from the film study clearly implicated movement as the source of the differentiating information. The nature of the movement difference was not clear in these films. We therefore decided to make a set of films that would focus on "pure" movement with no information from clothes or anything else. To do this we borrowed a technique originally devised by Johanssen (1973) to study movement in adults. Our models, boy or girl, were dressed in a black jumpsuit. On each joint a band of reflective tape was placed, one on each shoulder, elbow, wrist, hip, knee, and ankle. When filmed with appropriate lighting, nothing is visible save the clips of light from the reflective tape. On any frame of such a film, nothing can be seen save the twelve dots of light marking the position of the twelve joints.

The resulting pattern of dots on a single frame is not obviously human, much less girlish or boyish. In movement the situation is different. Even adults can tell that the moving figures are babies, although assignment of gender is far from perfect in most cases.

If these films are presented in pairs to babies, the familiar pattern emerges, with boy babies looking more at boy babies and girl babies looking more at girl babies. There is thus information about gender, information that babies can pick up, even in films composed of 12 dots of light.

Analysis of all of our films of babies moving indicated that there are some very simple clues to gender that even adults can rapidly notice. First and simplest, when a baby bends to pick up a toy, boy babies almost invariably bend from the waist, whereas girl babies almost invariably bend from the knees. Second, given a boy baby and a girl baby of the same height and leg length, the girl will take significantly shorter steps, 20 percent shorter on average, than the boy. One can, with careful editing, eliminate the first of these clues and minimize the second. The resulting pairs of films still elicit highly preferential looking from babies. The residual information seems to lie in the relative joint movements; girl babies swing their hips and everything else more than do boy babies.

Two linked questions immediately spring to mind. How do these differences come about and how do babies become aware of them? To take the latter question first, it would seem that babies are aware of their own pattern of movement. Presumably they are directly aware of their own patterning through information from joint receptors. What is more interesting is that they know what this kind of proprioceptively given pattern looks like in a visual presentation. This would imply that the perceptual system of ten- to twelve-month-olds retains the amodal or supramodal power of newborns, as manifested in newborn imitative behavior. This power has been thought to disappear very early.

The first question is one of nature versus nurture. Are little girls taught to move in a girlish way or does it come naturally? We suspected, for rather mundane reasons, that nature bears the primary responsibility. At the age we are currently discussing, there are virtually none of the anatomical differences between boys and girls that will be so obvious in later years. However, even at this age girls carry a greater proportion of their body weight on their hips. There is no difference in pelvis size, no difference in distance between hip joints, but girls' actual hips are 18 percent bigger than those of boys of the same overall size (Davenport, 1944). From a purely mechanical point of view, the weight distribution of girls will force them to swing their hips more than boys; compensating for the swinging hips will induce the relatively exaggerated, sinuous movements of the other joints. It might even be that compensation for the hip swing results in shorter steps, and that the lower center of gravity consequent on larger hips induces bending from the knee rather than the hip. The whole movement pattern difference might thus result from a biologically based difference in weight distribution.

That is not to say that there are no cultural effects. It is clear that there are cultural differences in the way adult women cope with the mechanical problems in walking produced by their own weight distribution pattern. Adult males in different cultures walk very differently as well, and it is not just a matter of belts versus suspenders. Adults could, by example or explicit correction, induce similar patterns in babies in that culture. Only cross-cultural studies of developing babies could answer this question and none have so far been tried.

My faith in this simple explanation, a biological difference with cultural modulation, was shaken, indeed shattered, when we tried to test it. Our test was far from perfect but was the best we could do. We recruited a boyishly built girl and girlishly built boy as models. They were filmed as before so that we finished up with two films of twelve moving dots of light. In terms of the crude factors we have noted before, there was no gender-appropriate difference. Step length and swing factors were the same. Despite this, infant subjects had no difficulty in picking out gender. The girl subjects looked more at the girl and the boy subjects looked more at the boy. The preference was reduced, to about 2 : 1 from about 3 : 1, but was still there. It thus appears that there is a difference we cannot yet categorize, perhaps to do with the fluidity versus jerkiness of girls' versus boys' movements. It is not obvious that this dimension could be biologically based, nor are possible cultural factors leapingly obvious.

Our interest in cultural factors has been whetted by studies of an infant behavior that shows gender differentiation where there is no possible anatomical difference to account for it. That behavior is the smile. There has been some controversy over what factors elicit the first smiles in babies, those that appear around six to eight weeks after birth. There were at least four competing theories, all mutually exclusive, all supported by experimental data. Some years ago I suggested that the source of the problem was our use of "the" in discussing smiling. It was at least possible that infants, like adults, had many different smiles, or at least four. Eventually this was tried out experimentally. Six- to eight-week-old babies were induced to smile in the situations said to be critical by the four competing theories. The resulting smiles were examined, for duration, frequency, and sequencing of component movements, to see whether the same behavior was elicited in the four situations, or whether four different smiles were produced, one specific to each situation. The results showed that there were four different smiles, each specific to one situation. That much we had anticipated. What we had not anticipated was that in each situation boys' smiles were different from girls' smiles. Figure 7–1 shows samples of the different behaviors.

In this case there are no obvious anatomical differences to mediate the different behaviors. That is not to say that there are no genetically programmed neural differences. However, it seemed worthwhile looking for possible cultural factors. Our starting point in this enterprise was our own adult criterion for what constitutes a smile. Right from birth, babies produce a vast range of facial gestures, many

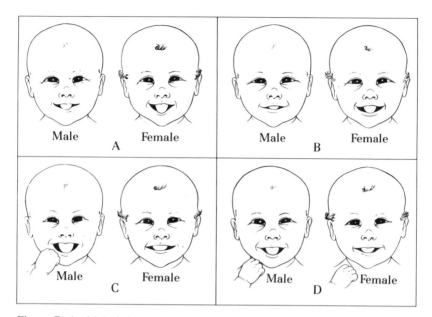

Figure 7-1   Male infants may have different smiles from female infants. (A) Contingency detection. (B) High-contrast dots. (C) The infant's mother. (D) A female stranger. (After Dunkeld 1978.)

of which look like smiles. They are not accepted as smiles, indeed are usually — erroneously — dismissed as the consequence of wind. Investigation of these gestures revealed that all of the eight different smiles found in six- to eight-week-olds occur in younger babies of both sexes in some form. The components are there, as is the sequence, but the duration is usually, but not invariably, much less. What happens to these early, charming but fleeting smiles?

Rather than carry out direct observation of maternal behavior in a real-life context, we took a large number of films of these smiles and showed them to heavily pregnant women or mothers of babies in the first eight weeks of life. We simply asked them to say whether the babies were smiling or not. Some of the adult subjects were given no information as to gender, some were told all of the babies were boys, others that all of them were girls. The last two groups were thus systematically misinformed, since the gender split was 50/50. The results were extremely interesting, showing that adult women have a clear idea of what is and is not a smile.

For our present purposes the most interesting result is that showing the effect of gender. Almost 50 percent of the facial gestures were categorized as smiles or not smiles depending on the supposed gender of the baby producing the gesture. A gesture, categorized as a smile on the assumption that the baby was a boy, would be dismissed as no smile if the assumption was induced that the baby was a girl, and vice versa. In other words, whether or not a baby is seen as smiling by an adult depends on whether the adult thinks the baby is a boy or a girl. We know that perceived smiles do affect the behavior of adults, particularly those adults who are parents of a young baby. What is likely to happen if a girl baby produces an acceptable girlish smile? She will receive attention, interaction, and every encouragement to repeat the behavior. Suppose the same girl produces a boyish — and therefore unacceptable — smile. She may then be thought to have wind, in which case she will probably be thrown over the parent's shoulder and buffeted about the body. This would not encourage a repetition of the behavior.

These two outcomes in fact give us a ready-made learning theory explanation of why the smiles of boys and girls are so different by eight weeks of age. It seems highly likely that adults' expectations are important determinants of the specific smiles that babies produce. If adults do shape one gender-specific behavior, there is no reason for us to think they do not play some role in shaping others, such as gender-appropriate walking (for details see Kujawski, 1985).

Indeed, I would go so far as to say that adults could shape the walking behavior of a baby long before that baby could walk. In the gender studies discussed above, the babies were able to match an abstract pattern of lights to the abstract pattern produced by their own joint receptors. I would argue that movement is centrally represented in a highly abstract form, quite different from the specific muscle twitches that mediate the expression of that form. There is nothing revolutionary in this view. If it can be invoked to explain maze learning in rats (Gleitman 1950), it can surely be invoked in this context. We can all of us accept that patterns of movement can be represented in an abstract form. How else would we understand Laurence Olivier's command to Marilyn Monroe, "Act sexy!" or a ballet tutor's command, "Move gracefully!" or a sports' coach's admonition, "Put more power into it."

How else, indeed, could we ever understand what method actors are talking about? Just as it is accepted that there are higher-order variables and abstract forms of representation involved in perception, so must we accept that there are equivalent abstract forms and higher-order variables involved in action. I have argued before that the perceptual system of the infant is more totally controlled by higher-order variables in perception than is the perceptual system of the adult: in the same way, I am now proposing than the motor system of the baby, *for* the baby, is characterized by abstract, higher-order forms of representation. I will not try to present a broad base of support for this proposition. However, there is evidence for it in the literature on operant conditioning. The onset of contingency detection produces an increase in movement of all kinds. The first thing the baby seems to learn is not "my leg makes the mobile move" but "my movement makes the mobile move." A switch of operant limb does not perturb young babies, showing that they still retain the abstract formulation of what is going on. It is not until eighteen months of age that we see systematic limb-by-limb testing in an operant situation, with anger if there is a shift of operant limb. Thus if adults reinforce a particular pattern of smiling, I doubt very much that the infant stores the outcome of *that pattern* as it would be described at a microlevel; it is far more probable, on the basis of everything we know about infants, that the baby stores something like "whenever I act girly, I get attention."

I would argue that in early infancy it is the most abstract possible description that is stored. Further it is clear that these abstract descriptions could begin to inform every act the baby executes. It is also clear to me that in a conservative country like Scotland, the behavior of baby girls is continuously monitored for "appropriateness" to the gender role, and it seems to me possible at least that the new behaviors of later infancy are gender-appropriate as soon as they appear. This has been remarked by others who have seen it as evidence of an unfolding genetic plan; since it is certainly not that—as Money and Ehrhardt (1972) have shown—it must, I would argue, reflect the effects of reinforcement of behaviors that have been abstractly described *by* the baby *for* the baby, described so abstractly that the description can program new acts, which will in turn receive more reinforcement. This would amount to an hypothesis about the correct way to behave, an hypothesis the baby could test without disconfirming it. If the reinforcement is positive, social approval by parents and if that is delivered noncontingently as well, we might expect high rates of gender-appropriate behavior to emerge as soon as the basic technology of the behavior is in place. The explanation I am offering fits with the cases described by Money and his coworkers as well as those of boys and girls with the normal chromosome patterns.

Gender is an important part of an individual's self-concept. It is, however, removed somewhat from the basic idea of selfhood, if there is such an idea. To get at this aspect of social development we have to look at imitation in infancy.

The developmental course of imitation in infancy has been a source of controversy for some years. I suppose the main point of contention for most people has been whether or not newborns can imitate. That point has never bothered me at all since the first time I was shown a newborn imitating, by Keith Moore (see Meltzoff and Moore, 1977), I have known they could do it. Since then I have seen hundreds of them do it. It is the most robust newborn ability I know. When passing film or TV crews want an example of an interesting newborn behavior, I direct them to imitation, invariably with success. Any behavior that is reliably manifested in the presence of a film crew — lighting man, camera man, sound man, producer, director, continuity person and the man who bangs the clapperboard — has to be pretty robust. My own worries were rather different. I knew newborns could imitate, but vaguely wished that they didn't, because the ability did not seem to fit with my ideas about newborn perception. Lastly, I was worried by my own inability to demonstrate imitation in any meaningful sense in elderly infants, infants between one and two years of age. I think I have now resolved all of my worries and I would like to try to persuade you that my resolutions are valid.

My first problem, remember, was whether the ability to imitate was compatible with my ideas about the perceptual world of the newborn. My core idea, briefly, is that newborns live in a perceptual world that is determined by amodal or higher-order variables, variables that are not tied to the particulars of one sense but which can be presented through two or more senses with equal effect. My views on this are presented at length in Chapter 2. The classic example of a higher-order variable is that determining our perception of radial direction. The variable is the symmetry or asymmetry of stimulation at our paired receptor organs. This variable is effective with our ears, nose, and feet (Békésy, 1967) and possibly our eyes (Bower, 1984).

Bekesy showed that the variable was effective in the absence of a normal sense organ, that perception via surrogate senses could occur, provided the same, abstract, formal, higher-order information was presented to the newly created sense. The newly created organ shared nothing with the other organs, at a purely sensory level: perception was driven by the higher-order variables that are invariant across senses. There is adequate evidence that newborns are sensitive to higher-order variables of this kind, more sensitive indeed than are adults (Bower, 1984; Aitken and Bower, 1982a).

For years I could not see that imitation was possible in this framework. For years I could not see that human movement produced, and could only be perceived by means of, higher-order variables. It took me a long time to realize that we can perceive human movement via the pattern of input from our own muscles and joints, and via a pattern presented to our eyes, the pattern being the same in both cases. The critical event for me was the patch-light experiment described above. Recall that in that study Kujawski and I (Kujawski and Bower, 1985) made films of babies moving, using Johanssen's technique (see p. 131). The babies had never in their lives seen anything like these films, at a sensory level. Nonetheless, first-look durations showed a clear same sex preference (see Table 2–2). How did they do it?

The source of the preference, it thus seemed, was the mapping of a pattern known via joint information onto a similar pattern fed in through the eyes. For such mapping to be possible without learning —and none of the infant subjects had ever seen anything like these patterns before the experiment—we have to concede that babies must be sensitive to higher-order variables specifying human movement, variables abstract enough that they can come in, proprioceptively or exteroceptively.

My problems with imitation clearly vanished at this point. Given that newborns have been making facial movements for some time before birth, they must be familiar with the patterning of facial movements. This alone would explain the fascination of visible faces for the newborn. Familiar patterns may be very comforting in the new world the newborn suddenly finds himself in. Imitation itself could be driven by a desire for the comfort of familiarity.

It seemed to me that a number of consequences flowed from these notions. First of all, what we call imitation should be as readily elicited by abstracted patterns of facial movement as by whole faces. Kujawski therefore reduced a face to a pattern of fifteen dots (see Figure 2–15). This pattern was presented to babies in a sequence of 90 seconds still face, 30 seconds moving face, 60 seconds still face,

30 seconds moving face, 60 seconds still face, and 30 seconds moving face, 60 seconds still face. Three gestures were used, wide mouth opening, mouth protrusion, and wide eye opening. "Wide" means the model's eyes and mouth were opened to their fullest extent, closing between gestures. Five gestures per 30 seconds were presented. Gesture order was counterbalanced across subjects. Subjects were in the second week of life. The tapes of the baby responses were scored by two judges. As Table 7–1 shows, there was a significant change in the frequency of each gesture during and for 60 seconds after its presentation in the patch-light pattern. There were few subjects, so this is clearly no more than a pilot study, but at least the results are in the right direction.

We have also compared imitation of the whole face of the mother with imitation of the patch-light displays. With infants in the first week of life there is no difference. They imitate both with equal facility. We are currently manipulating this kind of presentation to find out when the baby actually notices the transformation of his mother, there in full glowing color, into a pattern of fifteen dots.

It was Meltzoff who first saw imitation as an example of amodal perception. His analysis has generated a number of brilliant experiments, including one by Kuhl and Meltzoff (1982) which showed that infants could match a seen face to a heard voice. I am halfway through a replication and extension of this study. In the half that is done, Scottish infants were presented with Scottish faces and Scottish voices which matched, or mismatched, and also with Japanese faces and Japanese voices, matching or mismatching. All of the four-month-olds could match both. By twelve months, Japanese matching was impossible, the presentations evoking hilarity on occasion. The experiment is now under way in Japan, where we might expect the opposite decrement. This is an instance of experience producing a loss of competence, a stable loss of an early, if not innate, ability.

Table 7-1 Frequency of gesture following light-patch presentation

Presented gesture	Mouth opening	Mouth protrusion	Eye widening
Mouth opening	5.33	2.0	1.66
Mouth protrusion	1.16	4.0	.16
Eye widening	2.33	3.33	6.0

Source: Kujawski and Bower, 1985.

There are several other consequences that follow from this analysis of the perceptual basis of early imitation. One — which we have not tested — is that a still presentation of a frozen instant of a facial gesture should not elicit any imitation at all; a full-color photographic presentation of a face with wide-open mouth should elicit no special behavior. A second prediction, which we have tried to test, is that imitation should become less likely the more modeling presentations there are.

Imitation, I am proposing, is the reinstatement of a perceptual pattern, initially presented visually. One thing we do know about newborns is that they quite rapidly become bored with any perceptual presentation. If a gesture is presented often enough, babies could become so bored with it that they would not bother to reinstate it, just as, if presented enough times with a bull's-eye, they will refuse to look at it.

We have begun to try to test this hypothesis. Babies were presented with two gestures, mouth opening and tongue protrusion, for one minute each, followed by one minute of still face after each. The model was the mother. For one presentation, the mother was instructed to make the gesture every 5 seconds, for the other every 15 seconds. The former resulted in more or less continuous gestures, the latter in only 4 gestures separated by an interval of still face. Mothers were rehearsed on the gestures to ensure all took just under 5 seconds for a gesture. Each baby thus saw one gesture 12 times, and the other 4 times. Gesture frequency and order were counterbalanced across subjects. Imitation during the one-minute presentation and the subsequent one-minute still face were scored by two observers. Initially a mixed group of babies in the first and third week of life were tested. Table 7–3 shows the results for the younger group. It is clear that the more frequent presentation depressed the frequency of imitation although it did not abolish it. We plan to try this experiment more systematically, presenting gestures only when the baby is looking, trying to guard against looking away, and so on.

Despite its weaknesses, this pilot does indicate that frequency of presentation of a model will depress the frequency of imitation. Frequency in the general environment may depress the likelihood of imitation in an experimental situation. Indeed, some process like this may explain the difficulty of eliciting the gesture the newborn sees most often, the smile. Last year a television crew, unaccompanied by a psychologist, went into a maternity hospital and asked a mother to try to get her less-than-one-day-old baby to imitate her sticking her tongue out. The mother duly stuck her tongue out at her baby, grinning broadly between gestures. The baby responded by sticking his tongue out, interrupting the gestures with broad grins. The resulting film showed both gestures clearly. Whether the smiling was imitative, responsive or what, I do not know; it had the same profile as the classic gesture, tongue protrusion.

In the course of a variant of the second study described above, I noticed a characteristic of the imitation situation that may explain some people's difficulties in eliciting newborn imitation, and my own difficulty in eliciting meaningful imitation from one-year-olds. I was watching Dr. Jane Dunkeld (Stoppard, 1984) trying to elicit imitation from a twenty-day-old baby. It struck me that the baby's behavior was formally very like my own behavior, 30 minutes before, when I was varying reinforcement in an operant situation to try to discover the nature of a baby's understanding of a response-event contingency. Imitation experiments are quite like contingency-detection experiments. In both there are two events that succeed one another in time. In imitation, the events are the adult gesture and the infant gesture. On the analysis presented here, the two events are perceptually equivalent but occur with a temporal gap.

The identity of form, with difference in location, might make imitation a more interesting contingent-pairing than most of those the baby is exposed to. When we present a baby with a contingency, say between A and B, we manipulate the events A and B to try to discover the nature of the baby's understanding. We may introduce noncontingent reinforcement, or partial reinforcement; in the imitation situation the baby may do the same.

In these imitative games, the baby may discover a great deal, beginning with himself or herself. In imitation, a pattern seen to occur at one place in space is matched by a pattern felt to occur at a different place in space. Regardless of the modal properties — one event is seen; its match is felt — the baby will be aware that the two events are occurring at different places. In that, following Michotte (1963), lies the basic differentiation between self and other — like, yet unlike — that is the basis of all social interaction. Imitation presents the baby with self and other in a simple, clear way, simple enough that we could describe this most fundamental of social facts as a perceptual given.

What else might the baby learn by manipulating the contingencies in imitation games? In all of the instances of contingency detection that we have looked at, the baby was the operator; the adults provided the reinforcement. In imitation this is reversed. The adult is the operator and the baby provides or refuses to provide the reinforcement. Having watched very many sessions of imitation, I am certain that babies manipulate reward with us in the same way as we do with them. Suppose we look at tongue protrusion, *tp*. The experiment is of the form $Atp \rightarrow Btp$. Now the baby can and does stick his tongue out when the adult does, stick it out when the adult doesn't, refuse to stick it out when the adult does, and sit poker faced when the adult does. A striking instance of this occurred on the Miriam Stoppard television program "Your Baby." Dr. Jane Dunkeld was subject to schedule variations by an infant. Throughout it all, Dr. Dunkeld carried on protruding her tongue at regular intervals, with no evidence of disturbance. In this she was unlike a normal baby who would have shown some kind of disturbance. I would be interested to find out if adults who do not have a Ph.D. in experimental child psychology have the same cavalier attitude. If they do, the experience might speed the child's discovery that he is different from adults. Carried to extremes the baby might conclude that he and the other were different species, that the "other" was an alien. Stopping short of that, the infant would have a record for imitation of

$$Atp.Btp, \quad -Atp.Btp, \quad Atp.-Btp, \quad \text{and} \quad -Atp.-Btp$$

In other words the baby has the information required to conclude that $Atp \rightarrow Btp$ is both true and false, that is, irrelevant to anything else. The baby would thus conclude that imitation is an irrelevant behavior, if not worse (see Chapters 3 and 4) and can have nothing to do with anything else. And, indeed, in one experiment that seemed to be just what had happened. Babies between one and two years were required to imitate an adult in order to obtain a candy. Although very keen to get the candy they could not use imitation to get it. They could imitate but the projection, "imitation $\rightarrow$ get candy," did not occur, just as the logical arguments above would imply (Dunkeld, 1978). The ability to imitate was there but was not linked to the getting of candy. This functional isolation of an interpersonal skill recalls Bowlby's (1951) description of the affectionless character who may have considerable interpersonal skills that are isolated from the rest of his life.

I have poured a torrent of speculation into that last paragraph and would like to detail it at slightly greater length, so that you may decide whether any of the speculations have any merit. I am suggesting that imitation games can provide a search paradigm whereby the infant can discover a great deal about self and other. Note that I am saying only that it is a paradigm, not that it is the only paradigm. Infants can imitate at an early age. Nowadays every new mother knows that well and what baby imitates is a common subject of discussion and — dare I say it — competition between the young mothers I regularly meet. I suspect that mothers have always known that; Piaget's book on imitation (Piaget, 1951) contains imprecations against evil nurses who elicit imitation from infants who are "too young" in his terms. He clearly knew of the phenomenon just as clearly as he knew it did not fit into the theoretical framework he was then using. We may propose that infants normally have some opportunity to play imitation games, and always have had.

What can they learn from such games? The first given in any such situation is the existence and differentiation of self and other. Beyond that the baby can begin to define the parameters of self and the parameters of the other. Imitation games, I am arguing, give the baby the opportunity to explore the mind of the other, just as we psychologists explore the mind of the baby. Inasmuch as the other shows the same reaction as the baby, the other is like the baby. Inasmuch as the other behaves differently, the other is different. It is highly probable that some systematic imitation games will lead the baby to conclude that the imitation relation is of the form that we evaluated in previous chapters as "both true and false." Recall then, that any relation with that value is irrelevant to everything else; a proposition with the value "both true and false" can neither be asserted nor denied, and thus can never be put into relation with anything else. The baby might conclude that a particular imitative relation, say tongue protrusion, was irrelevant. On the other hand, I have argued throughout this book that the baby construes everything, every percept, every act at a more abstract, less detailed level than we adults would.

Given that a baby presented with the evidence that any tongue protrusion was irrelevant might conclude that the imitation of facial gestures was irrelevant or that imitation itself was irrelevant. Suppose the latter? What consequences would ensue? Suppose a baby who had construed his experience so that he was driven to conclude that imitative relations are irrelevant. That baby would still be able to imitate. However, that baby would not put any imitative relation into relation with anything else.

Now long before I had any reason to suspect that kind of explanation, Jane Dunkeld (1978) produced results that were exactly those predicted above. Her subjects were babies in the second year of life. All of them could imitate. In the situation in question, the baby sat on one side of a table, the experimenter on the other. In front of each of them was an identical pair of differently colored cups. The baby was restrained. The experimenter would pick up one of the cups that was in front of her, say a red one on her left. This would reveal a candy, which the experimenter picked up and popped in her mouth before replacing the red cup on her left. The baby was then released. What did the baby do? Did the baby pick up the red cup on his or her left? No. The most likely response was to go for the experimenter's cup. I will cut a long story short. With the best will in the world we could not even train babies to imitate in this situation, although all of them could imitate. Now this is just what the model given above would predict would occur; imitation is irrelevant and functionally isolated within the mind of the child.

The latter case reminds me irresistibly of the affectionless psychopath, an individual capable of charm but whose charming social ways are isolated, not linked to anything else. If we take imitation as a paradigm, we could readily imagine an infant learning social skills and learning that these social skills are irrelevant. The result would be an adult like the babies in the imitation experiment, someone who would not put their social skills into the context of their other needs, who would try to satisfy these needs directly, just like the babies in the imitation experiment. At this point we should recall just when an organism will be forced to evaluate a relation as irrelevant. If there is evidence of a relation between two events, and if the information given cannot be fitted into any simple form, then the relation will be evaluated as both true and false, fitting neither of the simple forms of understanding, $a \rightarrow b$ or $-a \rightarrow -b$ (see Chapters 3 and 4).

Such relations are incomprehensible in terms of simple logical forms. The term *incomprehensible* is not irrelevant in this context. I have observed a few individuals who had been diagnosed as psychopathic. Two of them became heated if accused of lacking emotion. However, neither could see what emotion had to do with anything else. They both claimed to understand themselves but to find other people incomprehensible. The psychopath as alien, uncomprehending, lost, does not exist solely in fiction, although Patricia Highsmith's Ripley does seem true to type. A child could learn that there was an incomprehensible relation between two events, an irrelevant relation. The child could learn that early, and then live with the consequence of the learning, an item of knowledge that could in principle never be altered. If there is any merit at all in the view presented here of how the infant construes events, then it might be that early in infancy we could see the emergence of general ideas of — or for — skills that are doomed to remain functionally autonomous throughout life.

I would like to stick with the idea of comprehensibility for a moment as we look at the last dimension of social development that I wish to consider, the development of the idea of personal efficacy. The ideas I wish to express have their links, most notably to the work of Seligman (1975) and Bateson (1972). However, for me they first emerged in conversation with John Watson. In fact I attributed the ideas to Watson in a talk in 1976 and in a paper in 1978 (Wishart et al., 1978). I was somewhat surprised when Watson (1985) attributed the ideas to me. I am sure that the disclaimers of paternity do not mean that the ideas are worthless.

The basic idea that I seized on is as follows. The baby, from birth, has a set of needs and desires to be satisfied. The baby has a small but growing repertoire of behavior with which to satisfy those needs. We can take it as given that no baby is ever successful in getting what (s)he wants 100 percent of the time. Some ends will be more attainable than others. Some behaviors will be more successful than others. The baby is involved in all of these relations. The baby could describe himself in his world with a set of equations that would all run "If I do . . . , then. . . ." Constant to all of them would be "I do." From all of these, the baby could construct in Watson's terms, or derive in mine, a sense of personal efficacy, a coefficient of how often he would accomplish his aims and how necessary he was to his aims. There might be subindices for specific behaviors, but there would be an overall coefficient of personal efficacy.

At one extreme we can imagine the environment described by Seligman (1975) and attributed to all young infants by Watson (1966) in his salad days, an environment in which the infant has no control over anything important. The outcome, as both of them have argued, would be "learned helplessness," a state in which the infant would have learned "I can do nothing," from which would derive . . . nothing! . . . in the way of action, or activity. Such environments do occur; their malign effects can be reversed (Watson, 1966) by changing the environment.

What of less severe environments, environments in which the baby is sometimes "sufficient" and sometimes "necessary" (Watson, 1985) in the attainment of his ends? In previous chapters I have argued that these means-end relations are incomprehensible and therefore will be evaluated as both true and false, and then isolated as irrelevant. I now wish to qualify that conclusion by adding a qualification about comprehensibility. If we consider any act-outcome situation, there is almost always a mass of other evidence that could modify the evaluation of the act-outcome relation. Consider visually guided reaching. Babies for months have problems getting their hand to an object. However, after a certain age they can see that they have missed an object and can take corrective action (e.g., McDonnell, 1975; 1979); similarly if an object is put in their hands they can see what has happened.

The act-outcome relations for the baby of five to seven months do not lend themselves to simple evaluation, unless the visual information above is taken into account. It would be possible for an infant to exclude noncontingent reinforcement, the placing of an object in his hand, from calculations of his own efficacy and necessity in that situation. In this, the sighted baby is at a tremendous advantage over the blind baby; while the act-outcome relation may be very similar on the surface, the information available to disambiguate what is going on is very different; sighted children do not show the precipitous loss of manual skills that is still seen in blind children. In this case I am talking only about information that is available. I presume that the infant at some point can use any information that we adults can detect as available to be used.

The inability to see what is going on must restrict the range of what the baby can understand. In social situations the baby will be unable to distinguish between occasions when (s)he is the focus of attention and when not, all of which will make the baby's world less comprehensible, with the possible consequences outlined in this book, consequences that match those described by various observers (e.g., Freud, 1944).

This kind of incomprehension need not result from handicap. It could result from inadvertent confusion, produced by caretakers. It could result from quite deliberate policy on the part of caretakers.

Bateson and Mead (1942) (see account in Bateson, 1972) have described the child-rearing practices of the Bali of their time. These practices seem designed to reduce the child to incomprehension about his or her act-outcome relations, to render them incomprehensible and irrelevant. This is, or was, a deliberate cultural aim since the culture they described viewed humankind as the plaything of the gods, discouraging any sense of personal efficacy or responsibility. The techniques described would result in the evaluation of relations involving self-induced acts as both true and false, an evaluation, recall, that can never be changed, thereby ensuring the cultural inflexibility that Bateson and Mead so bewailed.

This kind of cultural inflexibility would be another form of long-term developmental effect. In this chapter I hope I have convinced you that there is good reason to believe that early experience will have long-term effects on social development, and that we can understand how that would come about.

8

A Model of Development in Infancy

In this last chapter I would like to draw together the various ideas I have proposed in this book. I began the book with an argument that there are long-term developmental effects that should be of interest to psychologists; experiences occurring early in life can have effects at a great remove in time; the effects are powerful enough that they can override huge chunks of genetic information; the effects may involve new response systems and new stimuli. Part of the reluctance of some psychologists to accept that there are such developmental effects may stem from the difficulty of fitting these effects into conventional frameworks of theory. I have therefore tried to show that aspects of conventional theories might predict such developmental effects, and do provide some bases for understanding how early experience can have later effects on different behaviors. I have brought together a number of perspectives. The first line of argument, introduced in Chapter 2, was that the perceptual system of the young infant produces outputs that are more abstract, less differentiated than those produced by our own perceptual system. This idea itself is a decendant of the theory of perceptual development that I learned when I was a graduate student of Eleanor Gibson; that theory is no longer as heterodox as it was then. The second idea is that infants can learn at all ages. This notion was controversial in the early 1960s but is surely no longer so, complex learning in newborns being no longer thought worthy of particular mention (e.g., Mehler, 1986). The third point is that what infants learn and what they store is a function of what they perceive. I honestly do not think that the idea has been at all controversial since the 1930s. It follows from these ideas that the learning of infants will be more general, more abstract, less specific than a naive adult would expect.

It also follows that the learning of infants will show a natural, far transfer, to situations that are very different in terms of their specific content. An infant could learn and remember something about exterospecific stimuli, given inputs of sound; whatever was learned would transfer to inputs of light, since light, too, is an exterospecific stimulus. This is clearly a mechanism for long-term developmental effects. I further assume that infants and children, like other organisms, act in terms of what they know, what they have learned. The actions derived from a particular item of knowledge may protect the item of knowledge, and thereby render it impervious to change. One unfortunate experience could teach a baby that all members of the opposite gender are untrustworthy. That baby growing to adulthood would very likely act so that that piece of knowledge was rendered impervious to change, a long-term developmental effect.

My own favorite metaphor or model for what is going on is the development of the fertilized egg to yield an intact, functioning, adult organism. The nucleus of the fertilized egg contains all of the genetic information necessary to create a new, adult organism. That nucleus is preserved in every cell of the adult body, fingers, bones, liver, eyes, teeth, all at the core identical. They look and act very differently. What happens is that some input of information from the environment determines an undifferentiated cell to become a finger. Thereafter, the cell and all of its descendants take in from the environment only what is necessary to become and remain the cells of a finger.

Inputs that would permit the growth of eyeball, say, are totally excluded, not taken up, not used, not even registered much less transcribed. Learning in infancy has, I feel, the same embryonic power.

The next idea that I have used is that infants are rational. For me this is the most important idea in the book. It is the only one that I propose with any trepidation. In *Primer of Development in Infancy* I referred to the infant as thinking that something or another was the case. This provoked the ire of one reviewer of the manuscript to such an extent that I was forced to put in a disclaiming footnote, confessing that I was well aware that I could not prove that infants could or did think. That was about ten years ago. Today I would refuse to do any such thing.

The idea that infants are rational is not exactly novel. Piaget (1937) suggested similar ideas in his book *Origins of Intelligence.* The ideas presented here are in part derived from that book and from a paper Piaget wrote some forty-five years later (Piaget, 1981). The essence of the argument that I absorbed was that we can only say that an organism is rational if we can show that the organism operates on rational principles. A variety of systematic formulations of rational principles have been put forward over the last 2500 years. The study of these rational principles is the study of logic. To say that an organism is rational is to say that the organism is logical. To say that the organism is logical is to say that with a given set of inputs we have a determinate output from that organism. The output will depend on the precise logical structure of that organism. The explanation of input-output relations in terms of intervening logical structures has been going on for a long time. In the most general sense there is nothing novel or revolutionary in it at all.

It is important to remember that there are different logical systems. One can take a logical system and see what it would make of a given set of inputs. More probably one would program a microcomputer with the logical principles in question and look to see what the computer made of the inputs. We can give the same input to a baby and look to see what the baby makes of the inputs. If the outputs match, over an appropriately wide set of tests, we have prima facie evidence that would indicate that the baby operates on the same logical principles as those we have built into the computer. This computer modeling of infant intelligence is the kind of work, touched on in Chapter 5, that I have begun with Luger (Luger et al., 1983;

1984). I have no doubt that the computer will be able to mimic the baby. This, I would argue, is prima facie evidence that the description of the transformation system used by the computer is a first approximation to a description of the system used by the baby.

I will try to clarify what I am proposing and what I am not proposing. I am not proposing that the baby is a computer; indeed, I think that the human baby, the most powerful learning system in creation, is far superior to any computer. I am proposing that a computer can be made to mimic the behavior of a baby. The program for the computer can be represented by a set of propositions in a natural language, English. Inasmuch as the computer mimics the baby, that set of propositions is an adequate representation of what is going on in the mind of the baby. The key word is *representation*. We can surely represent what is going on in the mind of the baby without dreaming that the representations are really there. I cannot imagine ever thinking that a baby is a parallel processor, or a serial processor, or anything so utterly mundane, inexpensive, and probably made in Taiwan; however either of these might serve as a representation of the mind of the child, an unknown and unknowable reality.

In trying to work out a logic for the developing human I have, for the most part, relied on the kind of logic found in elementary college texts (e.g., Copi, 1961). The basic structure I have relied on is the "→" symbol, the symbol of what we mean when we use sentences like "whenever it rains, it pours." I have perfectly intelligent colleagues who dismiss any paper that contains such symbols. Fortunately for me I have found that my undergraduate students have no problems with these symbols, and some are, indeed, more at home with them than I am. Welford (1958) did point out that the ability to reason logically declines sharply in middle age.

The "→" symbol is of use in describing a situation of the sort encapsulated in the sentence above. One event occurs, then another event occurs. Is there a contingent link between them? Can we say that "whenever the first event (a) occurs, the second event (b) will follow," that is, can we say

$$a \rightarrow b$$

I have a longtime colleague who would stop reading at the line above. She is certain she cannot understand logic or mathematics or anything with symbols. I had considered dispensing with symbols and rewriting every symbol I have used in the book in common English. However, that would have made the book far too long and would have made me far too tired since I write in longhand only. I can only hope my readers did not have the same awful experience in primary school as my colleague.

Right! Suppose our baby has noticed a, then b. The co-occurrence of a and b, I argue, would trigger an hypothesis-forming mechanism in the mind of the child, a mechanism to account for this co-occurrence. The information given, a then b, or $a.b$, is ambiguous. "Nearer than" or "further than" is the most common ambiguity in space perception. In contingency detection, the ambiguity is between $a \rightarrow b$ (whenever a, then b) and $-a \rightarrow -b$ (unless a occurs, b will not). $a \rightarrow b$ is one hypothesis. $-a \rightarrow -b$ is another hypothesis. $a \rightarrow b$ says that every time a occurs, b will occur. b can occur without a, and it is of course possible that neither will occur. In the symbols we have used throughout, $a \rightarrow b$ means that $a.b$ can occur, or $-a.b$ can occur, or $-a.-b$ can occur. The only thing that cannot happen on this hypothesis, $a \rightarrow b$, is that a occurs without b; $a.-b$ must not happen. on this hypothesis.

What does $-a \rightarrow -b$ say? On this hypothesis a and b can occur. However, a can occur and b not occur, $a.- b$ and of course it can happen that neither a nor b occurs. The one event that must never happen on this hypothesis is $-a.b$, the occurrence of b without a.

The same core event $a.b$ is thus evidence for two mutually exclusive hypotheses. The baby, as I have argued, will seek to discover which hypothesis is adequate, and then will test the hypothesis, before accepting it (see Chapter 4).

If the baby does indeed go through this kind of hypothesis formation and hypothesis testing — and I am sure that the baby does — then the baby is indeed logical and rational. If I can convince my readers, or some of my readers, that the baby is logical and rational, only to the level discussed thus far, then this book will have been worthwhile. The importance of the theory of child development that is current among parents and other caregivers cannot be over emphasized; I would very much like to add to that theory the idea that infants are rational.

In the last 40 years, we have seen two revolutionary changes in the theory of the baby. The first, most directly due to Bowlby, although many others were involved, was the realization that babies have social needs, social needs as important as their physical needs.

Bowlby changed the world of the baby; every adult caregiver I have met knows that babies have social needs and tries to meet them. The unknowing emotional starvation that used to occur seem largely to have been banished (Harlow, 1962).

The second revolutionary advance in the theory of the child was the incorporation of the idea that infants are aware of what is going on around them, that they can see, hear, perceive. This all took place during my own professional life, which did interact with my life as a parent. It is clear that there has been a revolution in the theory of the infant; over the eighteen years since my youngest daughters were born, the theory has reached the marketplace. Eighteen years ago I could not buy in Scotland slings or seats or strollers that would allow a young baby to sit up and watch what was going on. There were no audiovisual toys with which the young baby could while away the idle hours. The market at that time expected babies to lie on their backs in a featureless stroller or crib contemplating a distant patch of ceiling or an even more distant patch of sky. Now your tiny baby, while awake and not actively involved with mother, will sit up in a well-designed chair, able to inspect what is going on, able to look at a variety of mobiles and other toys. The theory of the baby, what everyone knows about babies, has changed to that extent over eighteen years.

I would like in the same way to convince the world that babies are rational, that they can learn, and that what they will learn is a logical consequence of the inputs we provide. This kind of change in theory, applied at the level of the individual baby, could have effects as profound as either of those I have mentioned above. As an example of a possible change, I would offer the following anecdote recounted to me by a clinical psychologist working in an institution providing short-term (less than six months) care for infants and children. For reasons I will not go into, he assigned a nurse to spend a morning observing the other nurses in a ward of toddlers, particularly to count the number of times any nurse delivered positive or negative reinforcement to any infant. Negative reinforcement was defined as shouting, smacking, or forcible transporting a child. Positive reinforcement was speaking pleasantly, cuddling or playing with a child. Mealtimes were not included in the observation time. The results shocked the psychologist. The first sampling produced 96 negative reinforcements and 1 positive reinforcement. A recheck two days later, produced 126 negative reinforcements and no positive reinforcements at all. Some discussion with nurses then followed, with a final score taken two weeks after the first. That yielded 120 negative reinforcements and 1 positive reinforcement.

In terms of the information given, I would say that these babies were being given information to support the hypothesis "unless I engage in antisocial behavior, I will not receive any adult attention."* I am quite sure the nurses did not intend to teach this to the infants. Nonetheless, on the view presented here the babies could have come to no other conclusion. An awareness of the rationality of infants, an awareness of how they use the information we give them, would, I am sure, give pause to this well-intentioned but ill-advised behavior.

I can give another instance from my own experience. It concerned a young couple with a young baby who, they reported, had difficulty feeding. The baby would spend "hours" ingesting a single bottle. To cut a long story short it soon emerged that, although they were very loving and very caring parents, the only time they held the baby was during bottle feeding. The baby had detected this contingency and was hanging on to the bottle in order to be held. When the contingent relations in the parents' behavior was pointed out to them, they changed and the "problem" ceased. The problem may not have arisen had the parents been aware that the infant's cognitive system will operate on what it is given, just as its perceptual system will operate on what it is given.

The logical system outlined thus far in this chapter is the standard logical system used by all adults, taught in all introductory logic classes. Piaget (1981) at the very end of his life argued that it was possible that the infant, the child, and some adults might be able to use a less constrained logic than our familiar two-valued logic. I have belabored this point in successive chapters but will belabor it some more here. The logical system we are familiar with is highly constrained, constrained by the three laws of thought. Piaget (1981) proposed that the infant might well be free of two of these constraints. When I first heard this idea, I loved it, for all the wrong reasons. I loved it because it seemed to suggest that we could view the growth of rational thought as a process of differentiation and specification, just like perception. Be that as it may, Piaget was

---

*I give this form of hypothesis because I very much doubt that the staffing levels would be such that every instance of antisocial behavior was punished.

proposing that the baby could operate with a logic different from our own, but a logic nonetheless, with rational principles for inference and deduction.

The logic in question — relevance logic — discards the law of excluded middle and the law of noncontradiction. This means that it is possible to reason logically without the restrictions imposed by these two laws. That means that there are four possible evaluations of a proposition, rather than the two we are used to. A proposition can be neither true nor false, true, false, or both true and false. In this book we are concerned only with propositions — sentences — that describe a possible relation between two events. I am arguing that any single co-occurrence of events may trigger first a presumption that they are linked, and second, a testing routine to check the validity of the presumption. The presumption will get initial validation if, over time, it satisfies some simple relations.

In various chapters of this book I have talked about an operant situation in which a leg movement l produces movement of a mobile m. One co-occurrence of l and m, $l.m$, is sufficient, I would say, to provide a presumption that there is a relation between l and m. The presumption will be validated, if, over time the probability of m, given l, is greater than the probability of m, given $-l$, over the same unit of time, and if the probability of $-m$, given $-l$, is greater than the probability of $-m$, given l, over the same unit of time. That evidence would confirm that there was a relationship. However, it would not say precisely what the form of relationship is. The relationship could be of the form $l \rightarrow m$, in which case m can occur without l. It could be of the form $-l \rightarrow -m$, in which case l can occur without m. The information given, $l.m$ and $-l.-m$, is ambiguous about the two hypotheses.

At this point, any organism using relevance logic could only conclude that both hypotheses are neither true nor false. There is simply not enough information to say that either hypothesis is true, with the other false. I must emphasize again the linkage between the two hypotheses and their evaluations. Once our thinker has satisfied himself or herself that there is a valid relationship between l and m, the residual uncertainty is whether l ever occurs alone or whether m ever occurs alone. The instant one of these events occurs, the ambiguity disappears. Suppose there is a leg movement (l) with no consequent mobile movement ($-m$). Our rational infant can conclude that $-l \rightarrow -m$ is true; he can simultaneously conclude that $l.-m$ indicates that $-l \rightarrow -m$ is true, and that $l \rightarrow m$ is false. The assertion of the one is equivalent to the falsification of the other.

Similarly an occurrence of m without l is instant confirmation that $l \rightarrow m$ is true and $-l \rightarrow -m$ is false. The assertion of the value "false" emphatically does not mean that there is no relation between l and m. The awareness that there is a relation is what kicks off the whole process, and that awareness must persist.

Suppose, then, that an instance of mobile movement with no preceding leg movement has just occurred. "Aha!" our organism concludes, "$-l \rightarrow -m$ is false." Proceeding in a rational way to test that hypothesis, our organism might come across an instance where a leg movement was not followed by a mobile movement, $l.-m$. "Aha! that means $-l \rightarrow -m$ is true, but wait a minute, I already know it is false." An organism with ready access to relevance logic would simply evaluate $-l \rightarrow -m$ as "both true and false"; simultaneously giving the same evaluation to $l \rightarrow m$.

As I have continually insisted, this evaluation could have powerful effects in development. Any sentence about the relation between two events that is evaluated as "both true and false" cannot be put into relation with any other proposition or sentence. A sentence that is "both true and false" can neither be asserted nor denied. It must remain functionally isolated. It must also remain impervious to disproof, a permanent, isolated subsystem of knowledge. Clearly any such evaluations would have long-term consequences.

From what I have said, it would seem that long-term effects are pretty well certain to occur in most lives. I have not thus far made much mention of two other sources of long-term effects, stability. One is simple learning. Simple, straightforward learning will persist. In the United Kingdom some people over forty jump when an air raid siren goes off, even those who, like me, were only three years old when the war ended. The other, of course, is the theory of development held by the culture in which the individual grows up. Some theoretical ideas are so strongly and widely held that day by day, minute by minute, there are shaping and reinforcing signals emitted by all the adults in the culture. One widespread example stems again from Bowlby. There are children today from broken homes with the experience of bereavement. In my experience, caregivers expect these children to be maladjusted and are relieved when some evidence of maladjustment appears. This might in turn influence the child's behavior. On a small scale, while most texts on Down's syndrome emphasize the sociable, affectionate nature of these children, there is one which describes them as fiendish imps. Behavior in a care setting reflects the expectancies the caregivers brought from the text they had read. Our culture is doubtless permeated with beliefs so widely held we cannot even be aware of them.

If one can give an account of how it is that long-term, stable patterns in development can occur, can one use that account to do anything about those stabilities that are undesirable? If one analyzes a situation that has undesirable outcomes, one may be able to change the situation to avoid the outcomes that are undesirable. One attempt at this involved fitting blind babies with a machine called the sonic guide (Figure 8–1). Above, in Chapters 2 and 7, I have argued that much of the syndrome that characterizes the congenitally blind may stem from the child's incomprehensible relation to events in the outside world. The information available may lead the baby to conclude that his or her own behavior and all the relations involving it

Figure 8–1   A blind baby fitted with the sonic guide.

are irrelevant to anything else. The sonic guide is a new source of information. It should, in theory, provide enough information that these evaluations would not be made. Early results — and the oldest well-studied child is only seven — would indicate that the additional information can avert the undesirable outcomes (see e.g., Aitken and Bower, 1982a, b).

What of a child who has acquired some hypothesis or evaluation that is undesirable? Can anything be done then? In Chapter 6, I touched on a study designed to see if a "good" instance of far transfer could be restricted in some way. The argument there was that the infant given minimal experience with one situation will formulate a general hypothesis that applies to a very wide range of situations. If the child is given a lot of experience with the original situation, (s)he will refine and specify the general hypothesis until its contents are specific to the training situation; at this point there should be no transfer to new situations, no possibility of a long-term developmental effect.

To minimize the effects of a general hypothesis, I am saying we should present and overpresent the original situation that gave rise to the hypothesis, repeating it again and again and again until the contents of the hypothesis have been so specified that any other situation will be treated as a fresh field, without the malign effect that would carry over in the absence of the specifying experience. Please note that I am not saying that a child who has been abused by someone should be repeatedly abused until the experience is specific to that individual. I would assume that specification can take place without the complete sequence having to occur.

Let us take little Albert (pp. 50–53). He was taught to associate the sight of a white rat with a loud noise; the loud noise scared him; the sight of the rat thus induced fear. It was not just the rat that induced fear; any furry or hairy object induced fear. Albert had a general hypothesis about fur. I am certain that the generality of the hypothesis would have been reduced had he been given more exposure to the rat. I believe, too, that the benign effects of our training could occur at some remove from the original training, provided that the general hypothesis had not become self-buffering, self-reinforcing by that time. It may seem heartless to propose exposing a baby to a stimulus that induces fear. However, the procedure might reduce the fear intrinsic to the stimulus and would, I am certain, cut the possibility of transfer.

159

There is not much I can offer in the way of evidence for these therapeutic programs. However, I can offer yet another anecdote. A proportion of visually handicapped children have communicational disorders. They are not deaf, they can produce sounds, but they do not converse in any normal way. Some do not talk at all. This should not surprise us. Numerous authors (e.g., Butterworth, pers. comm.) have argued that joint attention, joint looking, is essential for, or certainly facilitates, the development of normal communicational skills. Be that as it may, the visually handicapped child clearly is at something of a disadvantage in working out the rules of conversation. One baby I knew found it so puzzling that she threw tantrums whenever adult speech went on around her. The tantrums were so awesome that the parents, while I was examining her, asked me not to speak but to communicate with notes, if communication was necessary. Needless to say her verbal communication became very poor indeed. It was a considerable surprise when this visually handicapped child, after years of speech therapy, took to sign language like a duck to water.

Teaching sign language to visually handicapped children sounds insane and yet it has exciting enough effects that there has been a European conference on the subject (1986). Teachers of the visually handicapped whom I respect are very excited about sign language as a way of communicating with those visually handicapped children who have such difficulties. It is possible that with years of training, the children have refined an original pessimism about communication to the point where it is specific to speech; they then seize upon sign language as something new, unaffected by previous malign experiences. This is but an anecdote but I think it gives us a hint about useful applied work we could do, if we want to. What we will accomplish in theory and practice will, I am certain, depend on what we can bring ourselves to accept of the idea that the infant we know so well, the beautiful baby we all adore, is, as well as all that, above all, a rational infant.

Bibliography

Aitken, S. 1977. *Gender Preference in Infancy.* M.A. thesis, University of Edinburgh.

Aitken, S. 1981. *Intersensory Substitution in the Blind Child.* Ph.D. dissertation, University of Edinburgh.

Aitken, S., and T.G.R. Bower. 1982a. Intersensory substitution in the blind. *Journal of Experimental Child Psychology,* 33:309–323.

Aitken, S., and T.G.R. Bower. 1982b. The use of the Sonicguide in infancy. *Journal of Visual Impairment and Blindness,* 76:91–100.

Alegria, J., and E. Noirot. 1978. Neonate orientation behaviour towards the human voice. *International Journal of Behavioural Development,* 1:291–312.

Alegria, J., and E. Noirot. 1978. Neonate orientation behaviour towards the human voice. *International Journal of Behavioural Development,* 1:291–312.

Amiel-Tison, C., and A. Grenier. 1980. *Evaluation neurologique du nouveau-né et du nourrisson.* Paris: Masson.

Anderson, J., and S. Belknapp. 1976. *A Theory of Logic.* New York: Wiley.

Attneave, F. 1959. *Applications of Information Theory to Psychology.* New York: Holt.

BBC ITV Enterprises. 1976. "Benjamin."

Ball, W., and E. Tronick. 1971. Infant responses to impending collision: Optical and real. *Science,* 171:818–820.

Bateson, G. 1972. *Steps to an Ecology of Mind.* New York: Ballantine.

Békésy, G. von. 1967. *Sensory Inhibition.* Princeton, N.J.: Princeton University Press.

Bower, T.G.R. 1966. The visual world of infants. *Scientific American,* 215:80–92. Offprint 502.

Bower, T.G.R., Broughton, J.M., and Moore M.K. 1971. The development of the object concept as manifested in changes in the tracking behaviour of infants between 7 and 20 weeks of age. *Journal of Experimental Child Psychology,* 11:182–193.

Bower, T.G.R. 1971. The object in the world of the infant. *Scientific American,* 225:30–38. Offprint 539.

Bower, T.G.R. 1974, 1982. *Development in Infancy,* 2nd ed. San Francisco: W. H. Freeman and Company.

Bower, T.G.R. 1977. *A Primer of Infant Development.* San Francisco: W. H. Freeman and Company.

Bower, T.G.R. 1978. *La préhension chez les bébés aveugles-nés.* Paper presented at Conference Anniversaire, Institut National de la Santé et de la Recherche Médicale, Paris, April.

Bower, T.G.R. 1979. *Human Development.* San Francisco: W. H. Freeman.

Bower, T.G.R. 1984. "Imagined Worlds." D. Cadbury, ed. BBC TV Enterprises.

Bower, T.G.R. 1985. L'enfant logique. *Bulletin de Psychologie* (in press).

Bower, T.G.R., J.M. Broughton, and M.K. Moore. 1970a. Demonstration of intention in the reaching behaviour of neonate humans. *Nature,* 228:679-681.

Bower, T.G.R., J.M. Broughton, and M.K. Moore. 1970b. Infant responses to approaching objects: An indicator of response to distal variables. *Perception and Psychophysics,* 9:193-196.

Bower, T.G.R., J.M. Broughton, and M.K. Moore. 1970c. The coordination of visual and tactual input in infants. *Perception and Psychophysics,* 8:51-53.

Bower, T.G.R., and J.G. Paterson. 1972. Stages in the development of the object concept. *Cognition,* 1:47-55.

Bowlby, J. 1951. *Maternal Care and Mental Health.* Geneva: World Health Organization.

Bryant, P.E., and T. Trabasso, 1971. Transitive inference in children. *Nature,* 232:456-458.

Bullinger, A. 1977. Head orientation of neonates in presence of a visual stimulus. *Année Psychol.,* 77:357-364.

Butterworth, G.E. 1978. Review of *A Primer of Infant Development. Perception,* 7:363-364.

Butterworth, G.E. 1982. *Joint Looking and Language Development.* Paper read at I.C.I.S. Austin, Texas.

Butterworth, G.E., and M. Castillo, 1976. Coordination of auditory and visual space in newborn human infants. *Perception,* 5:155-160.

Caron, R., A.J. Caron, V. Carlson, and L.S. Cobb. 1979. Perception of shape at a slant in the young infant. *Bulletin of the Psychonomic Society,* 13 (2):105-107.

Changeux, J.P. 1985. *Neuronal Man: The Biology of Mind.* Translated by Garey. New York: Pantheon.

Chomsky, N. 1980. On cognitive structures and their development. In *Language and Learning.* M. Piatelli-Palmarini, ed. Cambridge, Mass.: Harvard University Press.

Cohen, L.B., and E.R. Gelber. 1975. Infant visual memory. In *Infant Perception: From Sensation to Cognition,* vol. 1. New York: Academic Press.

Copi, I.M. 1961. *Introduction to Logic,* 2d ed. New York: Macmillan.

Darlington, R.B., J.M. Royce, A.S. Snipper, H.W., Murray, and I. Lazar. 1980. Preschool programs and later school competence of children from lower income families. *Science*, 208:202–204.

Davenport, C.B. 1944. Morphogenetic differences between boys and girls. *Proceedings of the American Philological Society*, 88:1–375.

Drever, J. 1955. Early learning and the perception of space. *American Journal of Psychology*, 68:605–614.

Dunkeld, J. 1978. *Imitation in Infancy*. Unpublished Ph.D. thesis, University of Edinburgh.

Dunkeld, J., and T.G.R. Bower. 1980. Infant response to impending optical collision. *Perception*, 9:549–554.

Etienne, A. 1972. The behaviour of the dragonfly larva after a short presentation of a prey. *Animal Behaviour*, 20 (4):724–731.

Festinger, L. 1957. *A Theory of Cognition Dissonance*. Stanford, Calif: Stanford University Press.

Fodor, J. 1975. *The Language of Thought*. New York: Crowell.

Fodor, J. 1980. On the impossibility of acquiring "more powerful" structures. In *Language and Learning*. M. Piattelli-Palmarini, ed. Cambridge, Mass.: Harvard University Press.

Fontaine, R. 1984. Tonus, posture, niveau de vigilance dans l'atteinte manuelle chez le nouveau-né. Colloque sur le développement cognitif el le traitement de l'information, Bruxelles, janvier 1984. In press.

Fraiberg, S., and D.A. Freedman. 1964. Studies in the ego development of the congenitally blind infant. *Psychoanalytic Study of the Child*, 19:113–169.

Gaze, R. 1971. Behavioural neural consequences of compound eye formation. *Centre National de Recherche Scientifique Bulletin*, 141:1–31.

Gibson, J.J. 1950. *The Perception of the Visual World*. Boston: Houghton Mifflin.

Gleitmen, H. 1950. Studies in motivation and learning. *Journal of Experimental Psychology*, 40:169–174.

Gopnik, A., and A.N. Meltzoff. 1987. The development of categorization in the second year and its relation to other cognitive and linguistic developments. *Child Development*, 58:1523–1531.

164

Gouin-Décarie, T. 1969. A study of the mental and emotional development of the thalidomide child. In *Determinants of Infant Behaviour,* vol. 4. B.M. Foss, ed. London: Methuen.

Gregory, R. 1963. Recovery from early blindness. *Quarterly Journal of Psychology,* Experimental Monograph Supplement, no. 4.

Gruber, H.E. 1971. Development of object permanance in the cat. *Developmental Psychology,* 4 (1):9–15.

Gunther, M. 1961. Infant behaviour at the breast. In *Determinants of Infant Behaviour,* vol. 1. B.M. Foss, ed. London: Methuen.

Guthrie, E.R. 1935. *The Psychology of Learning.* New York: Harper.

Guttman, N., and H.I. Kalish, 1958. Experiments in discrimination. *Scientific American,* 198:77–82.

Harlow, H.F. 1962. The heterosexual affectional system in monkeys. *American Psychologist,* 17:1–9.

Hatwell, Y. 1974. *Les privations sensorielles.* Paris: Presses Universitaires de France.

Hayes, L.A., and J.S. Watson. 1981. Neonatal imitation: Fact or artefact. *Developmental Psychology,* 17:655–660.

Hofsten, C. von. 1980. Predictive reaching for moving objects by human infants. *Journal of Experimental Child Psychology,* 30:369–382.

Hofsten, C. von. 1982. Eye-hand coordination in newborns. *Developmental Psychology,* 18:450–461.

Hofsten, C. von. 1983. Catching skills in infancy. *Journal of Experimental Psychology: Human Perception and Performance,* 9:75–85.

Hopeton, J. 1986. *Logic and Learning in Infancy.* M.A. thesis, University of Edinburgh.

Ikegami, K. 1984. Experimental analysis of stimulus factors in tongue-protruding imitation in early infancy. *Japanese Journal of Educational Psychology,* 32:117–127.

Inhelder, B., 2nd J. Piaget. 1958. *The Growth of Logical Thinking.* New York: Basic Books.

Jirari, C. 1970. *Form Perception, Innate Form Preference and Visually Mediated Head Turning in the Human Neonate.* Unpublished Ph.D. thesis, University of Chicago.

Johanssen, G. 1971. *Perceptual Organization and Movement.* Boston: Houghton Mifflin.

Johanssen, G. 1973. Visual perception of biological motion and a model for its analysis. *Perception and Psycholphysics,* 14:201-211.

Kagan, J. 1984. *The Nature of the Child.* New York: Basic Books.

Kellogg, W.N., and E.L. Walker. 1938. An analysis of the bilateral transfer of conditioning in dogs. *Journal of General Psychology,* 18:253-265.

Kosok, M. 1976. Dialectical Logic. *Human Development,* 19:325-350.

Krechevsky, I. 1932. "Hypotheses" in rats. *Psychological Review,* 39:516-532.

Krechevsky, I. 1938. A study of the continuity of the problem-solving process. *Psychological Review,* 45:107-134.

Kuhl, P., and A.N. Meltzoff. 1982. The bimodal perception of speech in infancy. *Science,* 218:1138-1141.

Kujawski, J. 1985. *The Origins of Gender Identity.* Unpublished Ph.D. thesis, University of Edinburgh.

Kujawski, J., and T.G.R. Bower. 1985. Gender perception in early infancy. *British Journal of Developmental Psychology* (in press).

Laing, R.D. 1971. *Self and Others.* Harmondsworth: Pelican Books.

Lee, D.N., and R. Lishman. 1977. Visual control of locomotion. *Scandinavian Journal of Psychology,* 18:224-230.

Leslie, A.M. 1984. Spatiotemporal continuity and the perception of causality in infants. *Perception,* 13:287-305.

Leslie, A.M., and T.G.R. Bower, 1981. Self-perception: the missing dimension in cognitive development. *Revista Internacional,* 2 (5):1-31.

Lewis, M. 1982. Development: A Constructivist View. Paper presented at International Conference of Infant Studies. Austin, Tex.

Lewis, M., and J. Brooks. 1975. Infants' social perception: A constructivist view. In *Infant Perception: From Sensation to Cognition,* vol. 2. L.B. Cohen and P. Salapatek, eds. New York: Academic Press.

Lipsitt, L. 1969. Learning capacities in the human infant. In *Brain and Early Behaviour.* R.J. Robinson, ed. New York: Academic Press.

Luger, G.F., T.G.R. Bower, and J.G. Wishart. 1983. A model of the development of the early infant object concept. *Perception,* 12:21-34.

Bibliography

Luger, G.F., J.G. Wishart, and T.G.R. Bower. 1984. A further analysis of the object concept. *Perception* 13:131–144.

McDonnell, P.M. 1975. The development of visually guided reaching. *Perception and Psychophysics*, 18:181–185.

McDonnell, P.M. 1979. Patterns of eye-hand coordination in the first year of life. *Canadian Journal of Psychology*, 33:253–267.

MacFarlane, A. 1977. *The Psychology of Childbirth*. Cambridge, Mass.: Harvard University Press.

McGurk, H., C. Turnure, and S.J. Creighton. 1977. Auditory-visual coordination in neonates. *Child Development*, 48:138–143.

MacKenzie, B.E., H. Tootell, and R.H. Day. 1980. Development of visual size constancy during the first year of human infancy. *Developmental Psychology*, 16:163–174.

Mackinson, F. 1973. *Topics in Modern Logic*. London: Methuen.

Mead, M. 1942. The comparative study of culture and the purposive cultivation of democratic values. In *Science, Philosophy and Religion, Second Symposium*. L. Bryson and L. Finkelstein, eds. Conference on Science, Philosophy and Religion, New York.

Mehler, J. 1985. Language related dispositions in early infancy. In *Neonate Cognition: Beyond the Blooming Buzzing Confusion*. J. Mehler and R. Fox. eds. Hillsdale, N.J.: Erlbaum.

Mehler, J. 1986. *Recent Research in Infancy*. Rome: E.C.I.D.

Meltzoff, A.N., and M.K. Moore. 1975. *Imitation of Facial and Manual Gestures by Human Neonates*. Paper read at Society for Research in Child Development meeting, Denver.

Meltzoff, A.N., and M.K. Moore. 1977. Imitation of facial and manual gestures by human neonates. *Science*, 198:75–78.

Meltzoff, A.N., and M.K. Moore. 1983. Methodological issues in studies of imitation: Comments on McKenzie and Over and Koepke et al. *Infant Behaviour and Development*, 6:103–108.

Michotte, A. 1962a. *Consalité, Permanence et Réalité Phénoménales*. Louvain: Publications Universitaires.

Michotte, A. 1962b. La participation émotionnelle du spectateur à l'action réprésentée à l'écran. In *Causalité, Permanence et Réalité Phénoménales*. Louvain: Publications Universitaires.

Michotte, A. 1963. *The Perception of Causality.* Translated by Andover, Hants: Methuen.

Michotte, A., G. Thines, and G. Crabbé. 1964. *Les Compléments Amodaux des Structures Perceptives.* Louvain: Publications Universitaires.

Money, J., and A.A. Ehrhardt. 1972. *Man and Woman, Boy and Girl.* Baltimore: Johns Hopkins University Press.

Monnier, C. 1981. *La Genèse de l'exploration chez le bébé.* Lousanne: Presses Universitaires Lousanne.

Mounoud, P., and T.G.R. Bower. 1974. Conservation of weight in infants. *Cognition,* 3:29–40.

Nielson, I. 1978. "Visual" Development in Blind Twin Boys. Faculty Report, Psychology Dept., Glasgow Institute of Technology.

Page, H.A. 1955. The facilitation of experimental extinction by response prevention as a function of the acquisition of a new response. *Journal of Comparative Physiological Psychology,* 48:14–16.

Papousek, H. 1969. Individual variability in learned responses in human infants. In *Brain and Early Behaviour,* R.J. Robinson, ed. London: Academic Press.

Pavlov, I.P. 1927. Conditioned reflexes; an investigation of the physiological activity of the cerebral cortex. Translated and edited by G.V. Anrep. New York: Dover, 1960.

Peiper, A. 1963. *Cerebral Function in Infancy and Childhood.* New York: Consultants Bureau.

Perkins, C.C. Jr., and R.G. Weyant. 1958. The interval between training and test trials as a determiner of the slope of generalization gradients. *Journal of Comparative Physiological Psychology,* 51:596–600.

Piaget, J. 1936. *Origins of Intelligence in Children.* New York: International University Press.

Piaget, J. 1937. *The Construction of Reality in the Child.* London: Routledge and Kegan Paul, 1955.

Piaget, J. 1942a. *Traité de Logique.* 3 vols. Lausanne: Presse Universitaires Lausanne.

Piaget, J. 1945. *Play, Dreams, and Imitation in Children.* New York: Norton.

Piaget, J. 1947. *The Psychology of Intelligence.* Translated by M. Piercy and D.E. Berlyne. 2d ed. London: Routledge and Kegan Paul, 1951.

Piaget, J. 1955. *The Child's Construction of Reality.* London: Routledge and Kegan Paul.

Piaget, J. 1979. *La Contradiction.* Paris: Presses Universitaires de France.

Piaget, J. 1981. *Cahier l.* Geneva: Archive Jean Piaget.

Piaget, J., and B. Inhelder. 1955. *De la logique de l'enfant à la logique de l'adolescent: essai sur la construction des structures opératoires formelles.* Paris: Presses Universitaires de France.

Rader, N., J.D. Stern, 1982. Visually elicited reaching in neonates. *Child Development,* 53:1004–1007.

Reissland, N., 1986. Paper read at Second European Conference on Behavioural Development, Rome.

Richards, B. 1985. Constructivism and logical reasoning. *Synthèse,* 65:33–64.

Russell, A. 1986. *A day in the life of a Scottish Infant.* M.A. thesis, University of Edinburgh.

Rutter, M. 1981. *Maternal Deprivation Reassessed.* New York: Penguin.

Sander, L.W., and W.S. Condon. 1974. Neonate movement is synchronized with adult speech: interactional participation and language acquisition. *Science,* 183:99–101.

Scarr, S. 1981. *Race, Social Class and Individual Differences in I.Q.* Hillsdale, N.J.: Erlbaum.

Schonen, S. de. 1980. *Développement de la coordination visuo-manuelle et de la latéralisation manuelle des conduites d'atteinte et de prise d'object.* Travaux du Centre d'Etude des Processus Cognitifs et du Langage. Maison des Sciences de l'homme, Paris.

Schonen, S. de, and T.G.R. Bower. 1978. *The Understanding of Spatial Relations.* Paper presented at Biannual Round Table on Cognitive Development in Infancy, Paris.

Seligman, M.E.P. 1975. *Helplessness.* San Francisco: W.H. Freeman.

Senden, M. von. 1956. *Space and Sight.* London: Methuen.

Skinner, B.F. 1950. Are theories of learning necessary? *Psychological Review,* 57:193–216.

Skinner, B.F. 1953. *Science and Human Behavior.* New York: Macmillan.

Slater, A., V. Morrison, and D. Rose. 1983. Perception of shape by the newborn baby. *British Journal of Developmental Psychology* 1:135–142.

Slater, A., V. Morrison, C. Town, and D. Rose. 1985. Movement perception and identity constancy in the newborn baby. *British Journal of Developmental Psychology,* 3:211–220.

Spemann, H. 1938. *Embryonic Development and Induction.* New York: Hafner.

Spitz, R. 1965. *The First Year of Life.* New York: I.U.P.

Stoppard, M. 1984. "Baby and Co." Yorkshire TV.

Stott, D.H. 1959. Evidence for prenatal inpairment of temperament in mentally retarded children. *Vita Humana,* 2:125–148.

Stott, D.H. 1962. Abnormal mothering as a cause of mental subnormality — II: Case studies and conclusions. *Journal of Child Psychology and Psychiatry,* 3:133–148.

Thorndike, E.L. 1911. *Animal Intelligence: Experimental studies.* New York: Macmillan.

Tolman, E.C. 1932. *Purposive behaviour in animals and men.* New York: Appleton-Century-Crofts.

Trevarthen, C., P. Hubley, and L. Sheeran. 1975. Les activités innées du nourrison. *La Recherche,* 6:447–458.

Turkewitz, G., H.B. Birch, T. Moreau, et al. 1966. Effect of intensity of auditory stimulation on directional eye-movements in the human neonate. *Animal Behaviour,* 14:93–101.

Valvo, A. 1971. *Sight Restoration after Long-Term Blindness.* New York: American Foundation for the Blind.

Watson, J.S. 1966. The development and generalization of "contingency awareness" in early infancy: some hypotheses. *Merrill-Palmer Quarterly,* 12:123–135.

Watson, J.S. 1972. Smiling, Cooing and "the Game." *Merrill-Palmer Quarterly,* 18:323–339.

Watson, J.S. 1985. Contingency perception in early social development. In *Social Perception in Infancy.* T. Field and N. Fox, eds. N.J.: Ablex.

Watson, J.B., and R. Rayner. 1920. Conditioned emotional reactions. *Journal of Experimental Psychology,* 3:1–14.

Welford, A. 1958. *Ageing and Human Skill.* London: Oxford University Press.

Werner, H. 1948. *Comparative Psychology of Mental Development,* rev. ed. New York: International University Press.

Wertheimer, M. 1961. Psychomotor co-ordination of auditory visual space at birth. *Science,* 134:1692.

White, B.L., and Held, R. 1966. Plasticity of sensorimotor development in the human infant. In *The Causes of Behaviour,* 2d ed., J.F. Rosenblith and W. Allinsmith, eds. Boston: Allyn & Bacon.

Wiesel, T.N. 1967. Behavioural and neural consequences of sensory deprivation. New England Psychological Association paper.

Wishart, J.G. 1979. *The development of the object concept in infancy.* Unpublished Ph.D. thesis, University of Edinburgh.

Wishart, J.G., and T.G.R. Bower. 1985. A longitudinal study of the development of the object concept. In *Infancy.* P. Harris and G. Butterworth, eds. London: British Psychology Society.

Wishart, J.G., and T.G.R. Bower. 1984. A normative study of the development of the object concept. *Advances in Infancy,* 3:57–123. L.P. Lipsett and C. Rovee-Collier, eds. N.J.: Ablex.

Wishart, J.G., T.G.R. Bower, and J. Dunkeld. 1978. Reaching in the dark. *Perception,* 7:507–512.

Yonas, A., A.G. Bechtold, D. Frankel, F.R. Gordon, G. McRoberts, A. Norcia, and S. Sternfels. 1977. Development of sensitivity to information for impending collision. *Perception and Psychophysics,* 21:97–104.

Yonas, A., L. Pettersen, and J.J. Lockman. 1979. Young Infants' sensitivity to optical information for collision. *Canadian Journal of Psychology,* 33:268–276.

Index